of us have come to appreciate from her creative content online. *Unfollow Me* is a continuation of Busby's work and it is for this moment as well as the next. It demands a follow, a like, a heart emoji, and a reader who is not afraid to be floored by Busby's incisive take on so many old inequities that ghost us still."

—Darnell L. Moore, author of *No Ashes in the Fire:*
Coming of Age Black and Free in America

"Frank, incisive, brutally funny, and moving, Busby has a gift for vivifying the keenest cultural observations with cutting, unflinching prose. I devoured this book."

—Amanda Montell, author of *Wordslut* and *Cultish*

"*Unfollow Me* is an emotionally risky, trope-turning manifesto of a book. Whether she's writing a letter to white hippiecrites, describing the disassociation that comes with online personas, or exploring the hell that can be microfame, her excavation is distinctive and nuanced. Jill Louise Busby for President."

—Chloe Caldwell, author of
I'll Tell You in Person and Women

"*Unfollow Me* challenges how we think about each other and ourselves in a way that is nuanced, funny, and vulnerable. Reading this book is like listening to your smartest friend."

—Mia Mercado, author of *Weird But Normal*

Praise for *Unfollow Me*

"Jill lets us know out the gate that she ain't come to play. This book is real, raw, and unrelenting. Dark, satirical, full of brilliance and badassness. Now is definitely not the time to be unfollowing Jill." —Killer Mike

"For anyone who has ever heard they were too much, not enough, and right on time all in the same day, this book will assure you that you're not crazy. A pleasure, even in all its painful, powerful truths." —Meshell Ndegeocello

"*Unfollow Me* reminds me of just how much courage I lack. It forced me to challenge who I've presented myself as, and to confront the invisible but thick tether between irreverence and conformity, especially as it pertains to conversations and stances around identity and technology. Her voice is sharp, but what's sharper is the feeling that Busby is asking us to complicate our arguments and muster up the moxie to sort and see our many selves in a more honest light. And for that, I am grateful."
—Jason Reynolds, #1 *New York Times* bestselling author of *Miles Morales: Spider-Man*, the *Track* series, *Long Way Down*, and *Stamped*, a collaboration with Ibram X. Kendi

"Jill Louise Busby has gifted us words that sing on the page with the insightful, poetic and witty euphony that many

UNFOLLOW ME

UNFOLLOW ME

ESSAYS ON COMPLICITY

JILL LOUISE BUSBY

BLOOMSBURY PUBLISHING

NEW YORK · LONDON · OXFORD · NEW DELHI · SYDNEY

BLOOMSBURY PUBLISHING
Bloomsbury Publishing Inc.
1385 Broadway, New York, NY 10018, USA

BLOOMSBURY, BLOOMSBURY PUBLISHING, and the
Diana logo are trademarks of Bloomsbury Publishing Plc

First published in the United States 2021

ISBN: HB: 978-1-63557-711-2; EBOOK: 978-1-63557-712-9

LIBRARY OF CONGRESS CATALOGING-IN-PUBLICATION DATA IS AVAILABLE

2 4 6 8 10 9 7 5 3 1

Typeset by Westchester Publishing Services
Printed and bound in the USA

To find out more about our authors and books visit www.bloomsbury.com
and sign up for our newsletters.

Bloomsbury books may be purchased for business or promotional use. For
information on bulk purchases please contact Macmillan Corporate and
Premium Sales Department at specialmarkets@macmillan.com.

This book is dedicated to my mother,
my brother, and you. Yes, you.

*Truth fights for itself. If you are open to it,
it will use you as a weapon.*

—JILLISBLACK

CONTENTS

UNFOLLOW ME

IDENTIFICATION

I am a black queer woman, and in case you haven't heard, I am having a moment. In this moment, it is more important that you know what I am than who I am. So I'll start there. I am an influencer. I am #BlackGirlMagic. I am a girlboss. I am diverse and I am included. I am an antiracist, radically honest, culturally relevant, intersectional womanist dyke. I am grant proposals and safe spaces and important new initiatives. I am self-care and self-love and self-empowering selfies. I am a national bestseller, a true triumph, an important story that will keep you glued to your seat and leave you in tears. I am the perceived expert of an experience, a fresh idea, a yardstick for liberal progression and conservative regression. I am a tiebreaker, a vote. I am just like you, but also, I am here to block you, drink your tears, cancel you from my cultures, and remind you that everything you have to say is irrelevant. I am in the room, seated at the table, holding a megaphone. And

I am so loud that all I can hear is my own feedback, an echo.

This is how I win now. Or at least that's what I'm told.

This book begins in 2016, when I was working in diversity and inclusion at a large nonprofit organization in Tacoma, Washington. Twenty-nine years old, with a frustrating lack of ambition, I mostly sat all day in my swivel chair, reciting rhetoric on conference calls and adding to the diversity of the place. Yes, I was selling my identities to the nonprofit machine, and no, it wasn't the first time. There were jobs where I led with my blackness, jobs where I led with my queerness, and jobs where I tried to lead with both at once. Before that, I'd spent five years working with my mother as a cultural competency trainer, scripting people and labeling their structural flaws as "misunderstandings." Often we just recommended team building. We were almost always invited back.

But I was growing tired of paycheck progressives, so like many people with a gripe, I uploaded a minute's worth of my feelings to my Instagram account. I called white people out for their intentional gradualism, their masking of a desire to maintain their racial status with varying displays of eternal naivete. I left myself out of it. The next morning a road had opened for me, and a choice about whether to take it.

Obviously, I made another video. And another and another and another. Soon there were offers to speak and write and I found myself with an inbox full of ego-pleasing options. My follower count grew by the tens of thousands and my face was all over specific corners of the internet. People called me by my social media handle instead of my real name when they met me in person. They asked for pictures and book recommendations and advice. One follower left the same comment underneath every video, encapsulating the appeal: "Jill is always black. And she's always on point, never off."

She was also, it struck me, the expression of a flattened identity, on repeat. I wanted to enjoy it, revel in the benefits like other identity influencers. I wanted to chase the headlines and react to them for easy content and more likes. But I couldn't. And after a year or so, I was just parroting the expectation. Following the rules I made. If you are interested in a book where I follow the trend and sell you an articulate account of my oppression, this book might disappoint you. If in order to see me, you must turn me inside out and be confronted with enough difference to make you feel privileged, then this book might disappoint you. If you are in search of an education that will ultimately allow you to know me better than I know myself, this book might disappoint you. And if you want to use this book as a reference to sound current and concerned at a diverse dinner party, it will disappoint. This book is not a comforting script or a way to win in a debate with a troll. I'm seeking something else.

I seek to go beyond cultural narratives and focus on what is universal about living in a world that quickly reduces you to either an exception or the rule. I seek to change the way we write about who we are so that we can stop mimicking each other for acceptance and personal gain. I seek the parts of us that can never be labeled. I seek to be on the other side of this moment. Yes, I seek truths about what it means to be black and queer and a woman in a dominant society that re-creates everything in its own image and calls it a success. But instead of avoiding my own compliance and accountability, I seek to aim the questions directly at myself, challenging the current narrative about race, gender, and sexuality and examining all the ways that I benefit from it.

I use stories from my own life to remind us that change is constant and growth is necessary, inside and out. (My mother has reminded me to tell you: The names of individuals who figure in these stories have been fictionalized. Any resemblance between the fictional names and those of real people is coincidental.) Ultimately, this collection is a look behind the curtain of identity, a search for the answer of why we fight so hard to stay so disconnected. It is an exploration of honesty, self, and ego and what exists beyond rage and being right.

Hi, liberal white people that like to name your kids after deciduous trees and maybe go to the local Unitarian church and also live in an unassuming and intentionally disheveled Craftsman-style house in a neighborhood that black people can't afford anymore. Hey. While you're here, I . . . I just thought I'd ask you a question. Um. I've always wanted to know. Like, but. How come everything's about you? Yeah, I just . . . I just noticed. 'Cause, like, even down in the comments, like, you're down there being like, "Oh, hey. Like, I . . . I don't mean to make this about me, it's just that . . ." And then you keep going and then, like, I mean, you make it about you. Like, everybody sees you doing it. And so I was just curious, like, how come, you know? And an example would be like, what is an "ethnic potluck," right? 'Cause that's an example of how you're at the center of everything and everyone else is just an "other." We're just accessories to your enriching cultural experience that you call life, where you just dabble in things and we're here to let you do that, right? *Yeah?* Well, if I'm here to just season your life, I'm going to make sure you're extra salty when I'm done.

—*Jillisblack*, October 6, 2016

STILL, UNTIL

How did all of this start for you? It's been four years since the beginning they mean, and since then, I have been asked this question more than any other. Wherever I happen to end up, it is always there waiting, always anticipating my arrival before I arrive.

The "all of this" they mean is my single gram of sub-demographic micro-fame on social media, and the "you" they mean is Jillisblack, which is the "you" that *I* perform on social media. The one who made the "Dear White People" videos and then later the "Dear Black People" videos and then later the "Dear Jillisblack" videos and then, soon, no videos at all. Because *I* can't do it anymore. Because *I'm* changing and *she* can't. Because I am an entire person, a much longer story, a more complicated answer. And because she's nothing more than a minute-long recorded performance of a truth that's always changing, a script that I've sloppily handwritten on copy paper or discarded receipts, an embodiment of the most comfortable parts of *my* ego, uploaded by *me* and fed until *she* is absolutely full of it by *their* likes.

When Jillisblack starts, there aren't as many versions of the same thing yet. Not as many bold characters using their boldest language to describe whiteness and what it does or doesn't do well enough for the kind of people who call it "whiteness." I go viral in the summer of 2016, and by the following spring I am one of a million versions of the same thing, "selflessly" building a platform off the artful articulation of collective anger and grief.

If I want to get shared, I have to go further and further, say more and more. I have to push the envelopes with the letters until I seem like the one who cares the very least about hurting anyone's feelings. If I post a video on social media and people's feelings get hurt, what I'm saying must be true. Because the truth hurts, doesn't it?

Social media can also turn on you, call you out for everything it had initially chosen to ignore or forgive you for. It archives what it has noticed about you for when you betray it. And I know that because I've done that. So I know I have to be careful.

The elephants in my room—my "obvious" proximity to whiteness, the fact that I haven't mentioned being queer since I became more known for being black (*who are you afraid to lose and why?*), my refusal (so far) to acknowledge the ways I benefit from colorism, my off-centered mouth and imperfect teeth, my unchallenged masculinity and who/what it could cause me to ignore, my lack of solutions, my need for internet attention, the fact that I can never be as "woke" as *she* claims because she's so desperate to claim it in the first place (*and why is that, exactly?*), how I don't even have *that* many followers, for real (*so don't act like you're* somebody, *okay?*)—can begin to trumpet all at once.

When we feel betrayed by someone—even a stranger— suddenly we notice everything about them that was always there. Every elephant.

So, in the beginning, it was all about what I was willing to say as Jillisblack. Then it became about what I know better than to say as Jillisblack.

Jillisblack *can* call out white people (specifically and in general) and America as much as she wants. Jillisblack *can* question symbols of the black elite, celebrity and (social) media, respectability politics, capitalism, hope, and progress.

Jillisblack *can't* call out things people grew up loving or still love or feel represent them and their experience in the world—historical figures, fictional characters, singers, movies, cultural icons, influencers. Even if those things are actually using their money and support to bet against them, to make themselves rich or powerful, to buy their own safety. Even if those things are just extracting the biotic natural resource of their unwavering allegiance and depleting it in the process.

I know because I still love all the historical figures, fictional characters, singers, movies, cultural icons, and influencers that I feel represent me, too. And because no matter how good I've gotten at dealing with the trolls, I'm still not ready for a mass unfollowing.

I don't come close to one until much later, when I announce that I'm married. (Jillisblack can't announce that I'm married.) Some people unfollow because they think that my marriage makes me complicit in an agenda to destroy the black family. Some people unfollow because they think that my marriage makes me complicit in a heteronormative construct that reinforces tradition and capitalism. Other people unfollow for reasons they don't bother to tell me.

Jillisblack is a watchful negotiation of these rules.

*

SHE STARTS ON a Friday afternoon, in the parking lot of a TwinStar Credit Union. I'm there to pick up my five free checks for the month and record a video for social media. So far, my posts have been about being high or broke or one because of the other. Or they're about the slightly alternative dating rituals of the slightly alternative and highly ritualistic. Or the common social media practices of exclusive friend groups, bougie and brunching in Brooklyn with grad school tote bags full of travel-size natural hair care products, gently motivational weekly planners, and deteriorating music-festival ticket stubs. Or the unspoken rules of the hip black queer community, inescapably connected by years and years of inner-circle dating and early internet reliance. All the things I know or am, say and do, want or act on. All the mirrors that allow me to see myself in public. And the critique that's accurate only because it's really just a confession.

I'm not fashionable, but I make an honest attempt—mostly when I know I'll see some of you, and/or I know I'll be photographed somewhere that is social-media-worthy, or when I have a photoshoot with a photographer who posted asking if anyone was around today to be shot in profile in front of a brick wall or a bridge.

But if I could figure out how to get away with wearing Eddie Bauer graphic tees and flare-legged khakis for the rest of my life, I would, y'all. Or rather, I would dress exactly like I did in the sixth grade, but forever. The only reason I don't is because I know that these days I'm actively attempting an image. And I know that my chosen image comes with a uniform. An aesthetic of sorts. It's how we identify each other in public/at a Drake concert. I know that I must fully engage with my hair. I know that my bold prints and patterns must be layered and plentiful. I know that my jewelry must be wooden and African and from Etsy. I know that my A Tribe Called Quest T-shirt must be showcased. I know that I must wear outfits that allow for full-body mobility in case I need to quickly share an article or request a Lyft to meet a friend for tea or do some yoga. I know that I must look like I just got back from a life-changing trip to Iceland or like I'm about to go to a music festival where Erykah Badu will be closing or like I just finished watching *Love Jones* in a college sweatshirt while eating an acai bowl at all times.

I get it.

But this video is different. This day at work has been particularly frustrating, and I'm sick to death of all the good intentions and best practices and identity expertise. I'm tired of programmatic care and fixing something from a distance and the soft whine of gradualism as it stretches to make itself more comfortable in my body.

This time, I'm sitting in my car, in the rain, clutching a few notes about white liberalism and the performance of trying and an eternal promise of *soon*, almost. And the notes are scrawled on the back of a return envelope for a bill I can't yet afford to pay, and the rain is almost too loud for what I have to do, so I wait.

But I don't know how to wait anymore without checking my phone. So I move through a series of evolutionary ticks: text messages, WhatsApp notes, Facebook notifications. Then there's Instagram, Instagram again, Google Chrome. My last search was "how tall is Brandy?" I already don't remember the answer. But, wait. It's right there—5' 7".

Also, she's an Aquarius. Which makes sense, even though I don't really know Brandy like that.

But don't I, though?

When I'm done, I check my work email. There's nothing from the large nonprofit where I am employed as a diversity and inclusion educator, no missed call from either of my bosses. They don't look for me when I arrive late or leave early, because that's what they do, too. Being mostly unaccounted for is part of the organizational culture.

And when one of my bosses happens to be in the office long enough to see my miserable corner cubicle, dark and unoccupied, my chair tucked, and it seems like maybe I should be there, *doing* something, my answer is always the same—I'm working remotely.

Even if I had been sitting in that corner cubicle, watching the rain through the one-way window, there would still be only the performance of work, my seemingly transfixed eyes staring at an old email until it was time to go home.

I was hired to ensure that the regional offices were following up on their elusive diversity and inclusion efforts through a variety of in-house training and quarterly committee meetings. I quickly learned that my actual job was to enthusiastically agree with everyone in upper management (via email, Zoom call, or in-staff training) that everything that could be done to make the organization more diverse and inclusive was already well underway. All remaining issues were budgetary, not behavioral.

It's a job that could be completed in an hour or two a week, but I manage to perform the remaining thirty-six or so hours into a full paycheck.

White people, you're always educating yourselves. When do you finally just . . . get it? Because black people have had to learn you so quickly in order to survive, so I know it's possible. Tell me, why is it taking you so long? Why is it so hard? Why is it costing you so much money?

9

Why do you need so many workshops and trainings and seminars and talks and panels and so . . . much . . . *time?*

When the rain finally lets up, I record my video and get it right in exactly three tries. Then I filter it, caption it, hashtag it, upload it, refresh it.

Okay, two likes. I sit in my car until the first comment comes in. Refresh again. Okay, it's good. They like it. They've noticed my haircut. They've tagged a friend.

Good, okay.

I spend five more minutes watching, waiting, refreshing, reading. Then I get out of my car, walk through the rain, and kindly demand my checks.

*

THAT NIGHT, EVERYTHING is the same. I cook dinner in my family's low-income apartment, turn on the music, call everyone in, and we all grab our food and gather. It's me, my mother, my brother. There are also two matching vapes filled with legal Washington weed for me and Chris, a glass of red wine for my mother. We sit around the long table that we inherited from a stranger and eat our vegetables, talk about nothing, speculate about the government or lack thereof, talk about money or a lack thereof, laugh. Listen to the screaming children who live next door with their screaming parents, and look out at the view of Mount Rainier from the tiny deck.

If only this could be enough for me, for what I want and what I think I'm supposed to be at twenty-nine years old. If only I didn't need so much attention all the fucking time. If only I could stop romanticizing my own displeasure, disinterest, distance.

But I was going to do something bigger than this one day. Beyond it. Something that wasn't diversity and inclusion work for an oversize nonprofit. I was going to finally reach my full potential and stop relying on tall tales of its existence.

I can't die selling my identities to an oversize nonprofit. I just can't.

So I disappear into my bedroom, with the stark white walls and the thin carpet, collapse onto the futon, and check Instagram. The video is doing well and I'm almost offended because why this one? Why now?

It isn't even funny.

But also, fine. This is okay, too. As long as someone knows what I mean and tells me so. Because that's what this social media is about for me—being heard, understood as some curated version of who I kind of am. So maybe this one is the right one after all.

*

SATURDAY, I WAKE up to twenty thousand more followers on Instagram and a text message from a friend who lives in Oakland, California. She links me to the video I shared yesterday, but now it's on Facebook, too. It sends me into a small panic, the reality of my face and my words escaping from the pen. A reminder of how uncontainable the internet is.

My friend is excited, warns me to probably stay out of the comment section. But like, *whoa*, dude! That's *you*, she says.

Congratulations. *You're everywhere.*

I tap the link and go straight to the comment section. I learn that I'm a fucking liberal, a victim, the problem with everything. I learn that I don't know what the fuck I'm talking about, that I'm an ungrateful nigger who should leave America since I hate it so much, a racist dyke who needs a dick in her mouth, a dumb bitch who needs to be taught a lesson. I learn that I'm overcompensating for not being black enough, the type we've all heard from enough already, thanks. I learn that I think I'm better/smarter than everybody even though I'm not.

Oh, and I should go fuck myself.

I also learn that I'm worthy of marriage, that I'm not bad even though I probably could've said it without the profanity, that I'm a queen even though I'm a little bit too masculine, a mix of Daria and Angela Davis (who knew?). I learn that I'm brave (on the internet) and important (on the internet) and that everyone should be required to hear me speak my truth (on the internet).

Over coffee, I tell my mother about it.

"So, you know I posted a video yesterday, right? On Instagram."

"Oh, okay. Uh-huh."

"Well, this morning I woke up and I have like thirty thousand likes on it and, like, all these new followers, and I—"

"Shit."

"Yeah, and a friend sent me a link to where it's been shared on Facebook—well, a couple of people have—and that link alone had over a million views already."

"Well, Jill, that's kind of a big deal."

"Yeah, right?"

I show her the video. I tell her how it started.

Just tell the truth, white people. Say that you'll never give any of it up. That you're flattered by the attention. By watching people spend their entire lives fighting for so much of what you already have. Waiting on a world you were—oh, shucks!—born into. Given. The one where the only downside—the only real bummer—is that other people must suffer in order for you to have what you want. The one where all of the numbers show you winning at a game where you're both a player and the referee. Tell me, do you think you got lucky to be born as you instead of me, or do you think it was God? And tell me, do you love being able to call yourself privileged when the only other way out is accountability? I have to tell you, what you see as privilege wouldn't be good enough for what we deserve.

She asks me how I feel and what I'm going to do.

But I don't know how I feel, so I ignore that part.

"I mean, I guess I make another video soon. I guess I keep doing it. I don't know."

But I *do* know. It's not the video I thought would do it, but the reaction to it is exactly what I've been waiting for. A chance to be more publicly appraised. A way out of anonymity and into visibility for saying stuff that I really mean. Actually believe.

I want to use Jillisblack. I want her to be honest without consequence. I want her to say everything about race and racism, power and privilege, hierarchy and hypocrisy that I can't say at work without getting fired. I want her to take risks I can't afford to take. I want her to speak without interruption, any way that she wants, for every time that I couldn't.

Maybe other people want to use Jillisblack, too.

So I spend a quiet weekend thinking about how to do it well. I study the comment section of the video. I make myself read every single one.

I strategize about how to avoid rhetoric traps and how to win against a troll without seeming like I care. I consider how to avoid the question of "But if what you're saying is true, what are you going to do? And if you're not going to do anything, then why are you saying anything?" I have no practical solutions yet, so I'll need good excuses. I think of what I should wear and how I should cut my hair and I come up with a rhythm for the recitation of the words.

I hide all the elephants I can and attempt to quiet the ones I can't.

And on Sunday, I sit in the parking lot of our apartment complex and record another video. Sit in the car and notice how quickly the likes come in now, the comments.

This is how all this starts.

Nothing and nobody warned me.

I think I'm using something against itself, but it's using me against myself.

*

A YEAR LATER, the Lyft driver asks you, "Why Harlem?" And it could mean a million things, really.

You tell him that you're going to a party, and that you always enjoy the ride to the party more than the party itself.

He laughs, says something about the pain of having to go places you don't want to go. Something about his son and his son's education. Something about moving here young, learning quickly, having to or else. Something about no regrets that sounds full of nothing but.

Eventually he remembers the radio, starts nodding along to the music, says, "It's a good night for a party."

It must be sarcasm or small talk, because the wind is whipping and the sky is full of deep, dark drama. People on the street—weary and accustomed—clutch their umbrellas like it's always fucking something. You watch closely like the visitor that you are, say to yourself for the millionth time something you already think you know.

Jill, you can never, ever live here.

Say out loud, "It's not that kind of party."

And you could mean a million things, really. But none of them quite matter. You want the beginning of the small talk that you've grown to adore, require. Circumstantial conversation with someone you're supposed to think you have nothing in common with. Happy to talk without talking *at* or in spite or in spite of. It's made you want something confidential and off record, and everything— absolutely everything—is on record now.

The people you sit next to on planes or share rides with become a break from the noise, an opportunity to drop the script and improvise. The more of these conversations you have, the more out of practice you realize you are with saying exactly who you are.

"Well, not a *party* party. An event, really . . . at Langston Hughes's house."

You know why you say it so specifically when less detail would do. You know that you don't need to, so you can't quite sell the words as casual. You immediately begin to worry yourself with all the possible implications of an unnecessary detail uttered aloud. What does it mean about you if you have to brag and pretend it's necessary for the story? I mean, it's Langston fucking Hughes, but who even cares, right?

You.

You care.

And you want him to care, too. You want him to care so much that it's worth the cost of a Lyft from Brooklyn to Harlem at rush hour. You want him to care so much that you get to convince yourself you told him for his sake instead of yours. You want him to care enough to be impressed.

He nods, merges, cares very little or not at all and goes, "Oh, okay. What's the event for?"

You quickly consider your options. Find that you both want to wave this line of questioning away like an accident you didn't seek out, *and* you want to be heard, to talk. To find out more about yourself from someone who is curious enough to ask you.

Not Jillisblack.

But Jill.

You.

Maybe you want to say, "I don't understand my life right now, okay? There were places and opportunities and circumstances that I wanted, sure. But I never actually believed that I'd have them. And now I'm in New York, in this car, on my way to someone else's idea of a party, and I have no idea what to do with myself. So, please. Just *like* me. I want to know that I still deserve it even when I'm not her."

Maybe you want him to think of you as different. Different from the other black girls who rely on the armored vehicle of social media to yell into the partially open windows of all the white people they used to worship who now just follow them. Those black girls who pretend their anger is wildly different from that of a scorned ex on a hot night, drunk-texting all their friends about how ready they are to move on while stalking the ex's comment section for reasons to stay mad. The ones who talk more about the ex than they do about themselves. The ones who can't stop talking about how much they don't care anymore. The ones who hope the ex is watching them not care.

Those black girls.

You.

So you say, "Um . . . it's for, like, people who other people think are going to change the world in some way. It's being sponsored by some publishing house, and you know what? I didn't even get my invitation directly. Someone got me on the list. So I'm not actually one of these people who's going to change the world, but I'm allowed to be around them for a night."

He smiles at you in the rearview mirror, proud like a father you don't have.

"Oh, I get to drive someone around who's going to change the world, huh? You should've said something earlier!"

You shake your head. "No, I'm not. In fact, I don't even do well at events like this. I feel out of place. I don't know what to talk about. I think if I were one of them—these people—then I'd probably know what to say to them, right?"

"Oh, don't even worry about that. They're going to love you."

You already know that they won't, but you don't want to disappoint him. Instead, you look out the window at New York—children dressed up as adults. Adults dressed up as adults. Custom assumed to be universal. Everything moving quickly, choreographed by predictable restlessness. A giving in to motion above everything else. As if things that are still or quiet can't change.

"It's not even that I want them to love me. I think I'd rather love *them* for once."

You say it quietly because it's a loud lie.

You do want them to love you. If they did, you'd convince yourself that you like them.

You want them to think you're brilliant. If they did, you'd convince yourself that they must really see you.

You want them to laugh at all your jokes. If they did, you'd convince yourself that they have a pretty good sense of humor.

But in case they don't, you were already skeptical before you ever arrived, right? You even have a witness.

"Fuck. I hear that. I hate *everybody* in this city!"

Your witness laughs, swerves. There's a lot of honking, but he doesn't seem to care.

You laugh, too, because you're scared.

"Well, these kinds of events are hard. Everyone just wants to talk about themselves and they look at your outfit while you answer their questions and you just stand around performing self-importance. We don't ever talk about who isn't in the room, you know? We just keep saying we need to get them in there. One day. Somehow. But do we invite them? No."

And if this is how you feel, then why do you go? Why do you choose the outfits so carefully? Why are you excited to finally be one of the invited? And why don't you ever stand in the center of the room and scream? Interrupt? Why don't you ever betray your own interests?

Since he doesn't know how you're meant to win the game you've chosen to play, he doesn't need you to be grateful for the party, the platform, the ounce of fame. The *micro*-fame. People who don't know your game sometimes give you too much credit for the way you play it. Sometimes they give you less because they don't understand how to win at their own. And sometimes they know the rules to your game better than you do. This is when they can sell you back to yourself for a price. Make you a trend you think you started.

Because he doesn't know, he says, "Are you happy doing what you're doing? Do you feel like it's important?"

"I guess. I mean . . . sure? Maybe not. I want to write a book, really," you tell him.

Sure, a book. If that's what's next, then yes.

That.

"Oh yeah? A writer?" he asks excitedly.

"Yeah, sure. That's why it's a good idea for me to be at this party."

"Hey, look. You got this. It doesn't really matter if you hate these people. You just go in there and get what you need from them. They want what you got and they got what you need, so fuck 'em, you know? Fuck 'em."

"I don't know if I need them yet, because I don't know what I want yet."

He can't listen because now he's talking to himself, too.

"People are out here for themselves. Period. You have to be thinking about you if you want to make it. You don't have to love the party. You just have to be at the party. Shit, sometimes you gotta *be* the party. But no, you don't have to like it. Just go in there and get yours. Fuck that."

"Is that how it works?"

"Hey, why not? And they invited you for a reason, so."

He shrugs.

It's easy.

You don't have to like the party.

"Yeah," you say quietly. But you're not sure. And you weren't even invited, really. You're a favor for a friend.

"Fuck 'em," he says again.

"Fuck 'em," you say for the first time.

But you win differently, so you mean it differently.

*

THIRTY MINUTES LATER, you find yourself standing in a room full of diversity efforts—two of everything that exists so far, like Noah's Ark. The preservation of identities. Intentional about it, though. Highly stylized, well traveled, and expensively educated, well on their way, their fantasies worth everyone's reality. Sometimes they're more honest one-on-one than in the art. But the art is the reason for the suffering and the suffering is the reason for the party and the party is the reason for the diversity, so it's good everyone could make it out in the almost rain.

You look around, trying to get a lay of the land, but then there are hands on your shoulders and you're being told by two grinning, staring white women—presumably from the publishing house—that they're so glad you could make it out.

Grinning, staring.

You find your name tag.

Still grinning, staring.

You grab a gift bag. There's a card, a book, a notebook. *Staring.*

Wait, now *grinning*, too.

They tell you to please help yourself to the table of food. Vegan fried something, vegan macaroni and something, vegan red velvet cupcakes.

And yeah, you're vegan, but not like this.

They tell you there's a bar. Yeah, if you head to the back where all the other people who need some help getting into character are standing. Straight back and to the left. Can't miss it.

Slightly nostalgic R&B music plays, and the representation nods its collective head on beat as it discusses its latest projects. And right in the middle of it all, watching from where it hangs above our heads, a painting of Langston.

After at least two awkward introductions, you start to get worried, frustrated. It has been a full ten minutes since your arrival and Jillisblack is nowhere to be found. You need her to shake hands, exchange the pleasantries that mean she'll do almost anything to get to the next level, exchange email addresses, smile like she needs this (because she does). You need her to pretend that everything is fine, simply because it's always the same.

You have a conversation with someone else instead. It's the most challenging of all the challenging conversations, and you're not sure whose fault it is. But also, it's yours.

For starters, you kind of look alike. She's the most obvious other you in the Ark. Moves her hands a lot when she talks, her wrists loose and concerned. She adjusts her glasses when she's not talking. Her hair when she is. She sips her champagne, watches you from behind her thick black frames. She makes her entire living emphasizing her points, and so far, all you have managed is some extra grocery money. She has a blog. Went to Columbia. She asks you if you've ever met Solange. That's when you know that she doesn't know that you weren't actually invited to this party. Not the way she was.

She asks what you do and then listens to you by saying "uh-huh" a lot. That's fine, because you're not doing a good job explaining what it is that you do. Mostly because you don't know what it is that you do. You know only what the thing you do does to you.

You have to explain it that way in order to explain it at all, and *that* way sometimes makes people scared for you.

"Um . . . I basically just. Well, I had a video go viral about a year ago . . ."

She perks up, "Oh, okay."

"Right, and I kind of grew my social media from there. I write these one-minute-long letters to white people, sometimes black people, or whatever, and I record them on video, upload them."

"Oh, okay. That sounds cool. But like, what are the letters about, exactly?"

"Well, I could lie to you and—"

"Uh-huh."

"Yeah, I could lie to you and say they're about white people or black people, but honestly, I think they're starting to just be about me. They're about parties like this and what I've learned by being at parties like this and what questions I have after parties like this. They're about all the things I haven't been allowed to say at work but now get to say online. So, I—"

"Uh-huh."

"I guess I'm also trying to get to the bottom of who we all mean when we say we're fighting for 'us.' Or at least when I say it."

"Uh-huh. Totally."

"Yeah."

"Do you deal with a lot of people being mad at you or a lot of trolls or whatever?"

"I have trolls from all sides. And they're all super angry and super scared, but for different reasons."

"Uh-huh, yeah. But I bet it's mostly got to be, like, racist-ass white people, right?"

"Um . . . sometimes, sure. But, I mean, there's also—"

She nods, turns to face the room, starts looking around for a person who isn't trying to figure themselves out in every conversation they have. It's not that kind of party. And anyway, she wanted you to say the right answer, to play the shared game.

You were supposed to call yourself an influencer, but roll your eyes at it just enough to suggest that it doesn't mean anything. You were supposed to say that you create content around race, power, and hierarchy, and when you're not filming content for a creative project, you're working on your book proposal.

Your book is supposed to be about your identities and what other people think about your identities and how you learned to love to write about them. Your book is supposed to be about being the token other and how you achieved personal success "in spite of" that token otherness. Your book is fourteen of your worst encounters with white people and a workbook they can use to help themselves not be the worst.

It could've evolved from there. She would've known what kind of business you're there to do, which rooms you're both in, and how you could either help each other, pretend to help each other, or avoid each other altogether. You could have made assumptions about who you are behind your interpretation of the same character. But your actual answer let her know that you don't yet know what you're going to do with yourself, and that makes you a dangerous person to network with or steal from.

Luckily, you're saved from her disappointment in you by a greater horror—as you almost always are. The person who got you on the list has arrived. She walks up to both of you after walking up to someone else first—of course. She smiles at the other you, hugs her. First. Then she slowly turns to you and says, "Oh, Jillisblack. Hello."

You used to follow each other online, ran into each other on another app. Sent each other text messages for a week. Then you got busy and stopped texting.

So, okay. There's a bit of tension.

It's your fault.

"Hello," you reply. "Nice to finally meet you in person."

She looks at your entire outfit from toe to head, tilts her head.

"I like your hat," she says with a smirk.

It means *fuck you* in every language.

"I like it, too. Thank you."

She smiles, but it's more like a dare.

Then she turns back to the blogger who knows what she wants and asks her questions about some news she's heard about her through the grapevine of doers. An opportunity, a deal. Something about Apple. Something about money—but they laugh about the money.

"We deserve to be compensated. These white folks have been cashing in on us forever. How much are they paying you? Oh, nice."

You still don't know the going rate of your identities in rooms like this. You don't know if you're selling yourself short. So you don't belong in the conversation. You walk away when you can no longer trust what you might say and before you completely ruin your chances of a future fireside chat with the popular blogger or a good word from the person who brought you there to both punish and promote you.

You never know.

You text your friend to let him know that you'll be ready to meet up much earlier than you originally thought. In fact, if he's ready now, that works, too. Yeah, he can just text you when he's outside. And in the meantime, you go get another drink from the bar and assess the room, try to find the best place to wait and hide.

Suddenly, you are jarred into immediate cultural confusion when Omarion's "Touch" begins to play over the speakers.

Why?

For *whom*?

Up until that moment, it had been all Sam Cooke and Boyz II Men, and this is something else.

You scan the room defensively, protectively. There is no DJ, so there is no one to blame, no irony to be found. Your eyes meet the photographer's—a middle-aged black man in designer glasses, wide-leg stonewashed jeans, and a fedora. He's standing next to his assistant, someone who looks like the girl from everyone's high school that was universally beloved for being both popular *and* nice.

The three of you look at each other, point in the air as if the song is playing in the atmosphere, laugh. And then eventually you give in, take the chorus together, insert the right choreography at the right time.

> *We cannot lose, just let it touch*
> *(Touch)*

For the first time that evening, you find overlap that isn't forced. A sameness that isn't just for show.

But there's another person in your periphery. One of the white women from the publishing house watches you with her hands folded neatly behind her back. She's the Noah who saved you from the life-threatening storm of your oppression. The only one with a boat big enough to fit a couple of everything.

She looks happy to see you having so much culturally authentic fun together, and you imagine her congratulating herself in a horrifying internal dialogue. She's gotten all of you here, hasn't she? You're dancing to Omarion under a painting of Langston Hughes, aren't you? This is a win, proof of her progressiveness. She can walk around a room of sparkling clean "BIPOC" and all the other letters that she uses to spell the same word. And you're eating the vegan fried something and telling each other about your very important work that's going to help everyone get free by winning an award and making (us) a lot of money.

You almost want to tell her with a careful knowing and wry grin, "Oh, hey. I'm queer, too."

This is alternative assimilation—a quiet compromise and a wide stance. Both feet in. And you've shown up in Harlem to mingle with the people who know Solange so that you might one day know her, too. To figure out how they earned their connections, their book deals, and their invitations so that you might one day have them, too.

So that you can say, "Wait, wait, wait. No, I think maybe we can fix it with representation and exceptionalism after all. I think social media micro-fame is totally a form of rebellion against the capitalist regime. As long as it's mine, it's justified. If it's someone else's, it's selling out."

And, you *do* want to write the book. You just worry that it comes with too many compromises, too many fake smiles, too many white hands neatly folded behind too many backs, too many personal brands. You worry that you'd have to spend too much time explaining your presence in the room.

And now you're worried that you'll have to write it as her.

But for the same reason you get your hair cut before filming a new video. For the same reason you "accidentally" say Langston's name aloud. For the same reason you don't stand in the middle of the room and interrupt, you'll write it.

You want to belong in a room of people who are going to change the world, who know what they want and how to get it. Isn't this the dream? Where you told your younger self you'd end up someday?

You find the bathroom and lock yourself in, stare at yourself in the mirror, ready for some straight answers. Ask yourself:

Like, is this it?

No, *stop.*

You.

Look at me.

Is this it?

Do you need to be applauded? Do you need to feel special? Do you want them to make you an offer you can't refuse? Is that what you're waiting for?

Is this really fucking it?

You say *progress*, but maybe you mean money. You say *unity*, but maybe you mean money. You say *revolution*, but maybe you mean money. Maybe you always mean money.

Will the money eventually get you to write the book that you wanted to write anyway?

What does the book even mean to you? What will you do to get it in people's hands? What will the gimmick be? What will you edit away that was too much, too soon, not palatable enough? How much money does the book have to earn in order to make you worth the risk? Will it be easier for them to just go with the book that the blogger who kind of looks like you is writing?

How will that make you feel?

Is she a more willing you with fewer run-on sentences and less trepidation?

What if it's not the money that scares you and it's not the money's fault? What if it's not the book that scares you either? What if it's you?

What if you're not ready to admit that you're already selling the identities, but for $45,000 a year and an annual conference in Denver instead of a million-dollar deal and two weeks' worth of vacation selfies in Bali?

You're already doing it.

Not having enough money isn't working. Can't you learn to love the rooms just until the revolution comes?

You're already doing it.

For an ounce more of fame and security, can't you be grinned at and keep dancing through it? Grin back?

Jill, look. You don't stop showing up to the party. That's silly and it's not the point of any of it. Your discomfort, your not knowing what you want, is more about you than anyone else. You don't stop ending up here. Here is where your work is. So you have to learn to trust yourself at the party. You have to know yourself in the room. Then, one day you confess about the parties. You write a book about the rooms that will make the rooms worth it.

You promise yourself in the mirror, and when you're done, you wash your hands. Dry them on your carefully chosen outfit. Return to the party like it's yours.

Fuck 'em.

Dear white hippiecrites,

You're here because you want me to remember that we're all human beings, living under the rule of a few evil men who love money, and when I focus on race, I'm losing sight of the real enemy. And really, we should unite against the capitalist regime and take our power back as a human race and stop being consumer-driven sheeple.

And, I mean, like, sure.
But here's the problem—like, you're so fucking racist.
You're so fucking racist.
And you always want race to be the first exception made in that list of priorities, you know?
So, here's the thing, hippiecrites. Like, I get it.
They're poisoning us and you're racist.
Excess is destroying our ethics and our planet.
And you're so racist.
Yup, me too. I'm a vegan as well.
And. You. Are. Racist.
So I think the question then becomes, like, when do you stop seeing me as a part of a culture that you can steal from to enhance your own supposed enlightenment? And when do you

stop just *backpacking* right through my actual existence?

Let's not play games with each other, hippie-crites. Like, you know, when you come here and you ask me, like, when am I going to see us as a human race?
I mean, like, after you.

[*softly*] As always.

—*Jillisblack*, February 8, 2017

A CONSEQUENCE OF US

I live in my grandparents' house for a year as an adult, in the add-on bedroom with the thick burgundy carpet and the king-size bed. In that room there's a walk-in closet filled with extra decorative pillows, holiday gift bags, broken things too expensive to discard, and dead insects. Holy and hanging on every soft-pink wall is a cross or a Bible verse, written in impressive calligraphy and hung with multicolored pushpins. This is my grandmother's way of reminding you that Jesus is hers.

Sitting below the crosses and calligraphy and sinking deep into the carpet is a collection of multigenerational furniture. It's so heavy and so settled that it will be hard to move when my grandparents die. I think about this often and feel dutifully guilty, as if it's wrong to remember that one day they won't be around. As if death is more untrue for them than it is for me or anyone else. As if the things we refuse to say aloud don't exist.

My grandfather is a deep rich brown. He loves Cadillacs and most gender roles. My grandmother is inexplicably pale. She loves indulgence and being sick. Together they love "get rich quick" business offers and Blue Bell buttered pecan ice cream. I know very early on in my life that they aren't like the grandparents from television or the books my mother reads to me at night. I know that they're mean. Their house doesn't smell like fresh-baked cookies *or* a pot of greens and their hugs aren't warm. But they do love Jesus. Jesus seems right for grandparents—even if my grandparents' Jesus is a bully who hates tomboys and loves new outfits.

That year, my grandparents call me instead of Him whenever they need something. They drag the *J* and the *i* of my name out across re-laminated floors and down hallways until it reaches my room from wherever they are in the house. By that time, the last half of it is always drowned out by the echo of the first half, over time making me miss the harmony of the double *l*'s at the end.

That year, I am called to fix uncooperative remote controls for uncooperative new televisions. I temporarily repair the printer that my grandmother uses for the weekly Bible study class she teaches at the nursing home. I spend hours on the phone with various customer service departments and order her the anti-aging face creams and the jewelry sets from the Home Shopping Network that she claims to need. I send new cell phones back to Consumer Cellular because the new ones never work right and the old ones didn't either.

It's the television's fault. The printer's fault. The phone's fault.

Strange.

Sometimes my grandmother calls me into her bedroom to try on clothes that she doesn't want anymore. I sit on her bed and listen to her tell me how much every item cost—again—as she covers me in a pile of Chico's women's petite size 2 blouses and pleated trousers. "I don't have anywhere to wear this now. Because you know at the new church, people can wear jeans and everything. You know those white folks don't care about clothes. Oh, and here! Take these, too. I got this set in all the colors they had because I liked it so much."

"You needed all the colors, huh? Just like . . . all of 'em?" I say from underneath the pile.

"Yes, Jill," she says. "I did."

"But you don't need them now?"

"No, now you need them."

My grandmother was once a teacher in the Oakland public school system. "I only taught in the flatland schools, you know, because that's where they needed the most help." Now, she thinks she's rich, watches Fox News, *Judge Judy*, and the Trinity Broadcasting Network all day from a couch where her small body is permanently imprinted into the cushions. She makes crude jokes when she thinks Jesus isn't listening, forgets to hide sometimes, forgets to be scared. She can't hear anything you're saying, refuses to wear the special hearing aid that cost more than the others. She says it makes everything too loud.

My grandmother remembers everything she wants to remember and discards the rest in prayer. She tells stories of the students from her classes in Oakland. She laughs at their reading levels and their sleep deprivation and the premature wisdom of forgotten children, forced to age right up out of their own bodies for survival. "Honey, those mothers could've done better. There's no excuse. And the children?" She slaps the table, shakes her head. "Some of them didn't want to learn. You couldn't do anything with them. They wanted to be on the streets like the parents, you see. And I would grab one of them by the coat—and honey, it would be so dirty I'd hate to do it—and I'd say, 'If you don't get your little criminal butt in that chair!' Sometimes, honey, I'd have to threaten them, because that's what they knew." She shakes her head again, then bursts into terrifying laughter.

I listen to her stories and I think to myself, "Jill, is this you, too? Are you more like her than you can see?"

I don't think so. But I can't figure out how I could've escaped it all.

Often some reminder of separation is necessary to sustain the black middle class, which is flimsy and circumstantial and unstable. The black middle class comes with lots of different identifiers and status symbols; there are many different ways to perform it. The most important thing is to know exactly which performance you can achieve from where you are and what you know. You try to spare yourself the embarrassment of thinking you're pulling off one performance only to have the people you believe are *your* people tell you that you're not one of them at all.

They think it's sad that you believed this lie about yourself.

Strange.

Or maybe hilarious, sweet. And sure, they'll point you in the right direction if you ask. They'll say, "I think that's actually your group right there. Just take the stairs down a little bit and make a left." You've just become their reminder of the separation they've achieved, and because you have your own reminders, you know exactly how little they think of you.

My grandmother uses the Oakland public school system as her reminder of the separation she achieved. She uses the mothers who worked all night at factories and the mothers who were neglectful because they were so busy self-defending and the mothers who did sex work to provide for their children as her reminders. She always mentions the one who would "do that kind of work" all night and drop her child off every morning. At first, my grandmother tells the story like she's championing the plight of the black woman, a life of always having to reach for what you need. But eventually, she just laughs. This mother will always be the butt of an untold joke. My grandmother thinks she's performed her way out of a type of blackness that is a punishment. A type of blackness that is sad.

Hilarious.

She could get away with being herself by buying herself out of accountability. For the black middle class, good parenting can be replaced by class ascension. So my grandparents paid for private schools and Cadillacs from the white dealership and lived as far in the hills of Oakland as they could afford. They bought an RV. My grandfather worked at General Motors and had a janitorial business on the side. My grandmother shopped at I. Magnin, enjoyed her evening screwdriver before bed.

Isn't this how the white people do it? Don't white people buy things, take things, and hide from their children? Don't white people act first, apologize never? Anything white people do first, the rest of us get to do next . . . right? A middle-class motto of "If it can't be good, at least it can be white."

But you don't shed blackness by shedding black culture. You simply end up like a black Russian doll, undressing out of yourself into infinity, always further within yourself to go. Either lost or found in self.

I live in my grandparents' house for a year, walking back and forth between my add-on suite and the office with the leaning filing cabinet, the old encyclopedias, the laminating machine, a closet of my grandfather's rarely worn clothes and photo albums with fading frills overflowing from the sides, and the drawer of blank cards and stickers. A room that smells of the 1970s, of overcompensation, of parenting better in photos than in practice, the glorification of the past. When I walk through the mostly carpeted house—a long walk, a long house—all the furniture makes noise, exhales in response to my steps. Nothing is balanced. Everything is made vulnerable by my presence.

In the office, my grandmother sits at the desk, recording all the paid bills on a sheet of paper, no wig, glasses low on her nose, draped in washed-soft cotton pajamas. When she speaks, it's in the dialect of the snobbish, judgmental black matriarch that we've romanticized. Maybe out of our own desire to escape the responsibility of kindness. Maybe because trauma made romantic allows us to still be in love with our community perpetrators. We shape them into types and defend the types instead of the people.

In the beginning there are more of us. There is a great-great-grandmother. There is a great-grandfather and great-grandmother. There is a great-uncle who is a professor, head of a black studies department, lives on a farm. My grandmother's brother. The one person besides herself that she can't ever stop talking about. He wears a cowboy hat and talks loudly, confidently. He calls my grandmother a *schoolteacher* on purpose. Tells her with a smug smile that it's okay that my grandfather didn't graduate from college, because he's so industrious. Good with his hands. A hard worker. His sister is his reminder of his achieved separation. But over time, people begin to die and take their side of the story with them. Lies get stronger in the one-sidedness of history recounted.

I live in my grandparents' house for a year and my grandfather and I don't talk much. He knows me more than she does. Not better, just more. People tell him things that they won't tell her. He knows bigger secrets. Sometimes we look at her and laugh. Neither of us feels guilty about it.

He likes to talk to me about the money I make when I get booked for a speaking engagement. It's not often, but it's usually enough to last me for a couple of months when it happens.

"They pay you that just to go up there and run off at the mouth, Jill?"

He means it in earnest, so I respond, "Yeah, they do."

He's kind of proud. I know because he says, "Well, alright then. That's not too bad."

"Nah, it's not too bad."

"How long you reckon you can do that job for?"

"I guess I can do it for a little while, Papa. But eventually, I'll have to do something else. I can't stay on the internet. I want to write a show or a book or something. Plus, it's not really a job, so . . ."

"Well, that's alright. That's alright."

"Grandmommy thinks I'm saying racist stuff for money."

He laughs. "Well, that's alright. As long as it's for money."

My grandfather is different from my grandmother. He loves money but not elitism. He likes when people are good at things without thinking they're too smart. He wants you to know that you aren't better than him and that he can tell when you think you are.

Sometimes he likes me.

I live in my grandparents' house for a year, with no job and no plan. But I could feel something coming. I was so sure of it that I wasn't even embarrassed to tell people that I was living in a room in my grandparents' house in Alabama, in a town I know better than any town in the world—buying my groceries at the Kroger twenty minutes away with twenty-dollar bills from my grandmother's thick billfold and the remaining money from my annual Black History Month gigs.

"Your event sounds great. When is it?" I'd respond to emails, already knowing. Already quite certain.

"Oh, it's in February!"

But because I'd almost exclusively offered up my blackness but not my gender or my queerness to popular media for money, I had a long off-season.

Black History Month was everything.

I live in my grandparents' house for a year, happy for months. I was reading every book about ego and consciousness that I could safely charge to my Discover card with the five-hundred-dollar limit and upload to my Kindle. Books about ego and consciousness written by people who had ended up exactly where they wanted to be, but then found themselves somewhere else. Spiritual teachers and former millionaires who had given up everything they knew for the pursuit of something more infinite. A God that isn't given. One you have to seek within yourself.

Because I had grown so used to a comment section, it was a relief to be called out on all my bullshit in such an intimate way. In my grandparents' extra room with the soft-pink walls and the sinking furniture that will be hard to move.

I still make Jillisblack videos in my grandfather's workshop because I'm not ready to let go of the ways social media has changed my life. Because I don't know how to live without the granule of micro-fame, the validation of likes, the heart emoji.

It's frustrating to feel happier without it and still think I need it.

My grandfather finds out that I'm filming in his workshop. One day he says to me, "Go out there and see if what I did works for that stuff you do on your phone."

In the shop, he's cleared out a space in the corner, hung a piece of drywall to use as a backdrop, moved a lamp and a chair in front of it.

I go back inside and thank him and tell him that it's perfect.

"Alright then. No big deal. Just took me about a half an hour," he says.

I live in my grandparents' house for a year, sad for days at a time. It would catch me right away, in the morning. I would know. It would take me over, talk to me in a condescending voice. "This whole place is doomed and there is nothing to look forward to. There is no impact big enough, and let's be honest, you'll never try anyway. You're scared and lazy. And look at you now. You can't even get out of bed. So weak that you can't even not be sad. Your ancestors didn't die for you to be *sad*. You must be one of those new blacks with the curated Instagram pages and the time for long captions. The new blacks stuck between generational goals, nestled in the reality of what they were supposed to want, in on a secret about what happens behind the closed door of capitalist progress but keeping quiet about it. You're weak. You're complaining about other people's problems. You're everything you critique. A moron. A traitor. Just as judgmental as your grandmother. Just as much talk as your father."

It would talk to me for two or three days at a time. And then one day I would wake up and forgive myself, remember myself, know myself again. I didn't know what to do with that other Jill, so I'd pretend not to know that she'd be back. Or sometimes I'd pretend that I knew the door she entered from and that I could close it whenever I wanted to, with enough green juice and exercise. But then I'd wake up on a Wednesday or a Saturday and know I'd awoken repossessed. "Good morning, you fucking hypocrite. What will you not be able to do for yourself today?"

I live in my grandparents' house for a year, in the moment. When I wasn't temporarily absent from my body, I was remarkably present in it. Rigorous in my seeking. If the books told me to breathe, I breathed. If the books told me to go sit in the forest, I would drag a lawn chair over the short bridge as my grandparents watched, confused, amused. I would sit in the middle of the trail that connects my grandparents' house to my aunt and uncle's house, across from a clearing in the woods where the birds would congregate for gossip and berries, and I wouldn't move. The trail that had not been made when me and my cousins were kids. We had walked along the street, enticing the cars with dancing and noise, unconcerned with consequences, in the moment.

One of the books suggests that I turn off most of the lights and stare at myself in the mirror until I start to feel disconnected from my body, from this reality. This feels important, since I had started being banished from it without warning. So I try it—once. After a few seconds in the near dark, I scare the shit out of myself with my own eye contact. Never try it again, decide it's less important than everything else because it isn't as easy as everything else.

It is from my grandmother and her fear of my queerness that I ever began to see it in myself. The way that I know it's real is that I can't hide it from her no matter what I do. Growing up, I watch myself carefully, try to adjust accordingly. But she knows anyway. She says I should be carrying a purse. I should always swing my arm in rhythm with my steps when I walk. It's more ladylike. I shouldn't be wearing jeans. But my girl cousins wear jeans, so I know it's just me who shouldn't and I know why. There's something suspicious about just *me*. And I shouldn't bite my nails either—it's masculine. Everything about me that's masculine is my mother's fault.

When I'm eight or nine years old, I figure out that people think that a lot of things are my mother's fault. This doesn't make sense to me, because my mother's smiles are real and she doesn't ask me to do anything ladylike or be anything I'm not, other than a little more quiet on Saturday mornings. She's funny and I can tell that she doesn't take any shit, so I don't either. She listens to me when I talk. She gets her hair cut into her signature short style at the barbershop, but sings Dianne Reeves songs while she sits on the couch and combs out my hair in our tiny living room. She buys me stonewashed jeans and on Fridays I get to rent a movie at Movie Gallery and sometimes—if it's payday—we get Little Caesars pizza. I love payday. I know that it's just the two of us and even though it doesn't feel like anyone's missing, everyone else can only see my father's shadow. I know that because she is a single parent, nothing counts. We don't count. Everything good about us is the result of something that should've never happened.

I live in my grandparents' house for a year and, once, I invite my future wife to spend the night with me in that room with the thick burgundy carpet and the king-size bed. I tell my grandmother that I have a friend coming by to see me and she'll leave late, out the back door. My friend and I are just working on a writing project together. No big deal. When she arrives, my grandmother spends an hour showing off her shelves.

In the living room that was once the carport, my grandmother has four rows of shelves where she displays family accomplishments—graduations, cars, vacations, old and new houses, certificates of recognition, photos of all of us when we're looking our most traditional or our most attractive. The only way you're described is by what you've achieved in capitalism or in class performance.

My uncle has the most real estate on the shelves because he's the most desperate for family approval and because he buys the most stuff. He has two sons but supports only the one who's desperate for *everyone's* approval. My uncle is always lonely, so he requires a lot of cheerleaders, flashy titles, and large suits. He talks a lot, makes a lot of promises, gives a lot of speeches, goes to a lot of events. Then he heads back home to sit alone in his big, empty house where the roof leaks and nothing is *quite right* up close. He sends my grandparents articles about himself filled with lies that they know are lies. They frame them and rest them on a shelf with the others.

One time he asks my grandmother to put me on the phone so he can get the number of a rapper he's heard I now know. It's the first time he's asked to speak to me in my entire life.

I manually drop the call.

I live in my grandparents' house for a year and one time my grandmother says to me, "What do they call you? Jill is black? Now why would they call you that? Since when are you black, honey?" She laughs and laughs and laughs. She smirks, loves and hates me in equal measure in moments like this. It's her way of reminding me that she's been here longer than I have, has seen more and less than I could ever imagine. We sit at the kitchen table, the seasonal plastic table cover noisy and sticky beneath our arms, and she laughs as I talk about us now. *Us*. Black people now. I update her on the trends, the news, the way we talk.

She says, "That's what y'all are doing, huh? They were doing all of that when I was a girl. Guess y'all think everything y'all do is brand new, don't you? Y'all trying to figure out how to be what you already are, huh? Well." She throws her hands up. "I guess you can't figure out anything else to do but be black. Honey, don't you already know you're black? The only people confused about it is y'all."

I can't deny it.

I live in my grandparents' house for a year and one day I find a Consciousness and Transformative Studies online graduate program. A school in California, of course. A school where I had done a semester and two days of law school years ago. Seems like a sign. The website uses all the words from all the books I'm reading day and night—the luxury of time, few needs, and my grandparents' house. I tell my grandmother I'm going to grad school so that she'll stop worrying that I'm a loser and so that I'll get a break from worrying that she's worried that I'm a loser. When she asks what kind of program it is, I lie to her and myself and stay intentionally vague. "Like, spirituality," I say. "Religion?" she asks. I nod, shrug. Sure, why not? What difference does it make? What harm does it do?

She starts to cry, calls my aunt on the phone at her office, tells the receptionist it's important. "Honey, you won't believe it! Jill is going to seminary school!" A blessing. Thank you, Jesus. She knew all along that one day it would happen. She knew that if she kept praying, I'd accept Him into my life as my one and only savior. Jesus knew, too. He always knows, and that's why they're friends.

In January, my grandmother gives me $100 and tells me to go buy a dress for my cousin's wedding. Well, first she gives me a $50 bill and I shake my head, remind her that I'll need shoes, too, of course. Or else I can't go. She says, "Yes, that's right. Because I've seen your shoes." She laughs and hands me another $50. The next day, I go to the thrift store and spend $15 on a mid-length black dress with long sleeves. When I try it on—which I do at home and not at the store because I don't quite care if it fits—I look like I'm in the "Addicted to Love" music video and everything about that is just right. Next, I go to the Dollar Store and I buy a pair of shoes that feel like they're made out of black construction paper, a two-pack of stockings, a brush. I proudly pocket the remaining $68, feeling like a winner.

The wedding is better with an edible.

There is a white minister from a campus church who reads everything from a book that might be the Bible. There are no vows, no stories told about how they figured out they were meant to be. There are no secret smiles, no tears, no nothing. He just reads from that book that honestly is probably the Bible, asks them to repeat a few lines back to him, and it's over. And when it's over, I feel victorious. Filled with righteous indignation.

There I am in that living room with all these people who
believe that marriage is sacred and the kind of love I've
found can never be sacred.

But I'm not done yet. I want more.

When it's time for the bouquet to be tossed, I already
know it's mine. I fight for it because I know they don't
want me to have it. And when I get it, I laugh and bow
dramatically. "Thank you, thank you!" I proclaim to the
people there who aren't my family. The ones who don't
know that I've ruined it. I wanted to ruin it, show how
silly all of it was. The pretense and the promises, all the
things that it meant to be married. The way *marriage* was
just a word for a kind of adulthood that so many people
choose.

I catch the bouquet and it's a bit of a disaster. The
whole family knows I'm queer, yes, but they ignore it.
I ignore it, too, for all the things it isn't worth having to
finally say. Yet we all know that there's something about
me—more things than one—that make this ridiculous.
My family is traditional, respectable, following along
behind the others, careful not to get too lost, and I am
too lost. What I am is too far.

In the middle of someone's speech, my grandmother
walks over to the piano and begins to play—loudly. My
cousin panics, widens her eyes at my aunt.

"Mama, get her," she says desperately.

When my aunt is finished sitting my grandmother
back down, they all have a laugh at her expense, and

I hate it. And I hate that I hate it. I spend the rest of the evening by her side like she's mine more than theirs.

I live in my grandparent's house for a year and in February I get married at a courthouse in Atlanta. The next morning, I drive back to my grandparents' house and respond, "Not much," to my grandfather when he asks what I did in the city. He knows whatever I say is a lie, but he doesn't say that. He just smiles, "Alright. Well, grab me the trash can out of your bathroom. Man comes tomorrow to get the trash."

He looks tired. My grandmother is worrying him, staying up all night looking for ways to sleep. I don't think I owe him anything, but I'm not quite sure.

I say, "Papa, do you have time to play a game of dominoes later?"

He smiles, shrugs, "Well, let me see. I've got to finish my yard, but after that I can probably beat you once or twice, ol' Jill."

I nod and go back in my room to get the trash can. By the time I return he's already forgotten that he's asked for it.

In that house, scriptures hang from the wall, the calligraphy menacing, a reminder of the black people they had fought to be. The black people with enough money to blow. Enough money to go to the white campus church thirty minutes away, enough money to talk about how black people need to do better, know better. But not enough money to desire freedom. Not enough money to not spend a significant slice of their time reminding everyone that they have enough money. Not enough money because there's never enough money and they don't have enough money to know there's never enough money.

I live in my grandparents' house for a year. It is a reminder of all that is sad and strange, hilarious and sweet. Separate.

A consequence of us.

DEAR YOU
(My Favorite Cousin),

There is a long house on a narrow street that winds tight around the trees that make for quiet neighbors, whose shadows stretch across the pavement like needy children begging to be held, and shade the threshold of a freshly mowed lawn, the crumbling concrete of a wide driveway, the edge of an increasingly false reality.

This is the house I know better than any other house in the world. The only house I will never be able to leave behind. Even when I leave it behind for the last time, finally meaning it for the first time. My picture still hangs on the wall, my image nailed through the fading wallpaper right next to a heavy interpretation of Jesus.

More trustworthy as a memory than as a reminder.

At least for now.

In this house, there is a room that I make mine for a year. But for a number of Junes, Julys, and Saturdays, many years ago, it was a room made for trying out discouraged things and trying not to get caught, the ears of the grandparents proving to be much less sensitive than the ears of your jealous sister and the mother she'd run to go tell.

You, cousin. We were the last two girls born before the boys started marching their way into existence, one after the next after the next in a single-file line, bringing with them significantly louder summers and the kind of cruel competition that is meant to mimic masculinity, prove it to someone.

We were born just months apart (you first) and made natural best friends by both choice and convenience. Our names were always paired, joined together in others' speech as naturally as the people they named.

In this room that was once ours, there are permanent stains on the carpet from the times it had no choice but to absorb the mishaps of our insatiable childhood clumsiness, all the spilling over and falling down. The lamp on the heavy dresser that sits underneath the window has a broken knob and we will always be the only witnesses to its final turn.

We spent our childhoods together making up stories for ourselves and for our dolls (you only had Barbies, and I only had Kens), making plans for who we wanted to be when we finally got old enough to decide for ourselves, making fun of the grandmother who was always making fun of us first—for our weight, our skin, our interests, our sins. We weren't old enough to make excuses for her, so instead we made jokes at her expense. The laughing made us feel powerful, the protagonists in our own fictional world. A world like the ones we saw on television, where brave kids win against everyone who wishes them harm. All the returning villains.

On television, there's always a villain, so having a villain is normal. The grandmother is the villain who wants to drag us back to Earth and spoil all the fun. That's normal.

We stay up until morning watching all the shows we're not allowed to watch and take turns standing guard at the door for when the grandmother decides to catch us in the act of being sinfully interested, lectures us for over an hour about the danger of seeking outside information, reminds us that Satan loves curiosity.

It's the door through which he enters the soul.

But we get older and Satan starts knocking because there is suddenly nothing more necessary than outside information. He's in the unmentionable details and shocking revelations of the aging that happens in private. He's in the tension that has started to underlie our conversations about boys, friends, proms, popularity. He's in the way the grandmother likes to pull one of us aside to tell us what the other has said. Asks if we know for sure that we can trust each other, after all.

The competition that we've always found ourselves in, fueled by dueling adults and the bets they placed on us to win, fueled by symbolic success and the price of its many secrets, fueled by gender and its role models, becomes all that there is between us.

Your parents are doctors and they never had to be anything but doctors. There are no requirements, no standards, no expectations from our grandparents because the doctors have done their part to make the family different, better. You and your siblings were sheltered to show that you could afford to be, so no one was allowed to mention it. How you didn't know how to answer the phone or go in the store to grab a loaf of bread or socialize without arranged activities. Your whining, crying, begging, failing—it was failure. Which is okay. Though we called it being spoiled, which isn't. And when you failed, you were reminded that you were the children of doctors, better than other black people whose parents had other jobs. Better than your cousin who didn't have a father. Better than the black kids at your church who went to the local public school with other black kids. Better than anyone who didn't have a pool. And when we fought in the summers, tired of all the free time and tired of each other, you would quickly make me your reminder of the separation. My mother may like me and we may have fun with each other and we may go to the museum on a Saturday with a packed lunch and a half tank of gas, but your parents are doctors. And the doctors don't have to like you.

And besides, everyone knows I like girls.

We don't have time to stand guard for each other because we're too busy learning how to do it for ourselves, against villains we never saw coming.

The year I live at my grandparents' house, I barely see you. When I do, you romanticize my life now. You need me to be the one who's okay. Need to make living unrealistic, something that only a few of us will ever get to do. I shake my head at this familiar game. I'm too old for it now. Not a teenager anymore. Too much has happened. Too much hasn't happened yet. Instead, I try to tell you that sometimes I'm sad and that the social media popularity isn't what it seems. The followers? Single gram of micro-fame. I don't know how I'm going to pay my bills and I don't know what I'm going to do with my life, and social media moves quickly, won't last forever. I have to *do* something. Look at me. I'm right next door to you. We're kids again and adults now and we're both right here together. It's not so funny anymore, the chaos that adults make. It looks different from inside. And some days I can't even open the blinds, stare at myself in the mirror thinking, "This is it? This is all you have for me?" But your reality is reinforced by your fantasy of mine, so you say, "Yeah, but . . ."

I am tired of *yeah, but*s and I am tired of fantasy.

We used to laugh about coming from a family of liars. A family whose social status is more supposed than actual, the illusion of it sustained by new furniture and old shams. But it's an illusion we think protects us from something. If we are believed to have enough money or education, a respectable-enough job or family, maybe we stay safe from the realities our grandmother says we can't handle. The ones she says aren't ours.

You get to believe in it more than I do, because it's pretending to believe in you. You weren't saved from the narrative by being the child of its underdog, an outlier. Yours was supposed to be good, right, better. So you never got to question it or see it as unfair, and you never had to fix anything that was broken.

Even through it all, even though you've stopped returning my calls or wanting to know what I think, even though the grandmother says the two of you have started to get very close, actually, even though I have become more circumstance than choice for you, there are still moments in that room—maybe on Thanksgiving our junior year of high school after we've been ejected from the formal dining room for laughing through the group prayer—that we are the protagonists, the brave kids.

There's the time you fall asleep with the news on and wake up to the sound of our phony uncle's voice on CNN, claiming that black people should be more concerned with silver rights than civil rights. We're in that room in the long house when you tell me, and I say, "No way!" and you say, "How could I even make that up?" and we both laugh until we cry, because of course. Of course he said it.

But then we get even older, and there is nothing under us to absorb our outcomes anymore, no one to laugh at except ourselves, nothing to blame on Satan.

For the year I am there, you are right next door. In the room that has almost always been yours. In the house that *you* know better than any other house in the world.

I can't make you text me back. I can't make us friends again. I can't make you want to visit me in that room.

I mostly see you if I need tampons and can't afford them. I cross the bridge and walk through the forest that sits between the grandparents' house and the house that you know best and ring a doorbell I've been ringing ever since I grew tall enough to reach it.

I'm always excited to see you, hopeful that this time you will surprise me, invite me in.

But every time, you meet me at the door, and there we stay while you cycle through your comedy routine about being a terrible cousin and an awful friend, before quickly sending me back through the forest and over the bridge with twenty or so assorted tampons wrapped in loud pastel-colored plastic. Loud familial silence.

In the house, there is still a grandmother and a grand-father. The grandmother still has her mind, and the grandfather still has his body. The grandmother still has her long-term memory, and the grandfather still has his part-time job. The grandmother still holds grudges, and the grandfather still holds his tongue. With age, their survival has become a joint effort, a group project with a major deadline. But maybe that's all it ever was.

We used to know who they were. We used to laugh at how far everything had gone, how unhappy they all seemed, how ridiculous we looked in our caps and gowns, sitting side by side on a shelf of grand spectacles.

We weren't supposed to take this on, continue it. We were supposed to know it well enough to disbelieve it, run from it.

The essay about living in that house for a year is how I'm saying goodbye to the narrative I know best. The room, the grandparents, the aunt and uncles, the cousins. All of it.

I don't want to lie and I don't want to compete. I don't want to repent for sinning in public. I don't want my picture mounted on a wall of unearned sacrifice.

The grandmother keeps asking me what the book is about. What I possibly have to say that's worth people's money, interest, time.

You and I used to be bound by all the things we couldn't ignore about that house, that narrow street, that false reality. So I'll tell *you* instead. Write to you out of everyone, because you are the only one I'll miss when the truth that we used to know, together, becomes mine alone. And you can be the witness to that cycle—the one where we name a family problem and inherit it out of fear—as it takes its final turn.

Love,
Jill

FLY HOME

I'm in Philadelphia to moderate "A Conversation on Race & _____." I touch down, take a Lyft to the hotel, talk to Marcus in a Black Infiniti QX60 about our '90s R&B favorites, know that I'll make him laugh if I mention "Last Night" by Az Yet, mention "Last Night" by Az Yet, laugh with him, arrive, tell him that I had a good time talking to him, too, check into the hotel and find my room on the fourth floor, choose to sleep in the bed closest to the bathroom, grab my phone, learn the hard way that it's *just a little* too late to still order Uber Eats, berate myself for eight to eleven minutes for not thinking to do it when I was still in the Lyft talking about Brian McKnight, console myself with thoughts of all the food I'm going to order the second I wake up, text my mother, unpack the basics from my backpack, lay them out on the extra full-size bed, remember that I have an apple in the front pocket, eat the apple while watching two episodes of *Catfish* on the hotel television, scroll through social media and get very mad at a person I follow but don't really know for disagreeing with me about something people disagree about, throw my phone on the other full-size bed, turn off the TV, try to remember why I'm so mad, remember and get mad about it all over again, brush my teeth in the stark white bathroom, stare at myself in the mirror, pull the shower curtain closed so I can see my hair better, have a fight with myself as if I'm both me and the person I don't really know who made me mad, win big against the weak arguments of my own reflection, get back into the bed I chose and turn the extra pillow sideways, turn off the lamp and reach for my phone in the dark, realize that it's still on the other bed, say "Fuck" to an empty room of myself, tell myself that I don't even fucking need it, accidentally think about social media and get mad again, say, "Fucking shut up about it already. We get it," to an empty room of myself, twist, turn, consider grabbing the phone, decide against it, try to fall asleep for two hours, twist, turn, try to wake up for three hours, notice that it's suddenly one hundred billion degrees in the room, walk over to the wall unit and turn on the air, grab my phone, check social media, feel anxious, remember that I can order Uber Eats, order Uber Eats and start to feel a little better, consider posting online that I'm in Philadelphia, decide against it, watch a marathon of *Cutthroat Kitchen* until Uber Eats arrives, walk down to the lobby in sweat-pants and a coat I wouldn't have packed had I antici-pated the heat, avoid as much eye contact as possible, retrieve two bags of food from Yvette, thank her, make my way back to my room with the two bags of food, open the bags and spread everything out on the desk so I can see it all at once, put half of it in the fridge and tell myself not to forget it when it's time to leave, sing three words of "I'm So Excited" for an audience of only myself, eat the other half of the food while watching *House* on mute, drink the carrot juice I ordered to feel like a lifestyle coach, text my mother, scroll through the notifications on my phone, scroll through the noti-fications on my social media, watch a video with a million views of a child hitting an adult in the face, scroll through the ten thousand comments, ignore the ones about how the child deserves what she has coming to her, ignore the ones about how she's a grown-ass woman trapped in a little girl's body, ignore the ones about how it would be kind of sad if it wasn't so funny, feel unsettled, throw my phone on the extra full-size bed, watch an episode of *Law & Order: SVU*, feel unsettled, mute the TV, call my mother, talk to her about how much I hate social media, listen to her tell me I don't have to do it, hear what I want to hear because I called to complain, hang up and look at the clock, take a quick shower under a weak stream of lukewarm water, get dressed, pack the basics back into my backpack, tidy the room, take a selfie, request a Lyft and make my way down to the lobby, spot Luis in a silver Dodge Durango and wave, listen to Luis sing Ariana Grande as I watch Philadelphia through the window, arrive very early, thank Luis and tell him that he has a beautiful voice, sit in a park for an hour watching people push strollers, walk over to the museum, meet the contact person and follow them to the room where the panel will take place, meet the panelists and listen to them talk about what they have in common, moderate the panel, finish and wonder if I was the best choice for the job, feel guilty about never being as "Jillisblack" as people are expecting, feel angry that I feel guilty for not being a 2D image of myself that lives on the internet (but only after four or five takes and a filter), thank everyone involved and request a Lyft, get out of there as quickly as possible, look outside for Meredith in a burgundy Ford Flex, spot her parked across the street and run to catch her before she leaves, throw my suitcase in the trunk and say a winded "Hello," spend the ride in silence, arrive, thank Meredith, grab my suitcase from the trunk and head inside, remember too late that I forgot my food in the hotel fridge, pull up my boarding pass on my phone, wait in line, show my license, take off my shoes, closed-mouth smile at anyone I make eye contact with, get patted down, find the one available electrical outlet at my mostly empty gate, plug in my phone, remember that I have work in the morning and set my alarm for 6 A.M., check Instagram, sigh.

Fly home.

Dear black revolutionary internet intellectuals,

Yo. Like, eventually there are only two answers. It's racism or it's self-hatred. It's *racism* or it's *self-hatred*. It's not really that complicated. And you can keep writing all of the things and saying all of the things, and when someone critiques you, you can do that thing where you bring up all the white schools that you went to and all the white publications that published you and validated your super complex feelings about racism and solidified your intellectual wokeness—which, *yeah*, totally a thing. White validation will always point us in the direction of revolution. I agree with you. *And* I think that you should continue to rely on the very systems that you're critiquing to explain why you're qualified to speak. *And* I think you should continue pretending that you can both separate yourself from black people and defend blackness. *And* I think that you should continue making money off of it, too, because what's a bigger motivator to fix a problem than to make money off of the problem existing? Like, what can go wrong there?

I'm even trying to think of an example of when exploiting black people for money went wrong for black people . . . Let me think of it.

Hold on.

. . .

I'll think of something.

—*Jillisblack*, January 15, 2017

THIS IS HOW IT STARTS

When they ask you how it starts, you know they don't mean the part that happened at Highland Hospital in December 1986, when your best friend birthed you into the world—or at least into a town called Oakland—and gave you your first and middle and last names.

Your father wasn't there, so neither his first nor last name appear on your birth certificate. You know now that your mother used to jokingly refer to him as "Mr. Withheld," among her friends. But never in front of you.

In front of you, he was named only by the position he still refuses to fill.

She was careful about him then. Not for his sake, but for yours. The first years of your life, you have no idea that fathers are supposed to be any different from the one you have, so yours is perfect.

Fathers are supposed to come around once in a blue moon with two other kids you don't really know but who are suddenly supposed to be your older brother and sister, because that's what your father does. Fathers are supposed to run your bathwater too hot and leave you (alone) in the tub to go talk on the phone, because that's what your father does.

Fathers are supposed to be a special occasion, because that's what your father is.

When you're four years old, your mother moves you both to Alabama because she needs to raise you somewhere else. Somewhere slower but with longer days. Somewhere more affordable than Oakland already isn't in 1990. You try to miss your father but you don't know how to do it. Missing him is what reminds you that he exists at all. How do you miss him differently from that? From farther away than never close?

When cable television and public school have forced you to trade in the comfort of your own fallacies for the pressure of the collective ones, you have no choice but to start asking questions. You gather up the courage (or the necessary disappointment) to want to know him beyond the character both you and your mother have created in his place, the cardboard cutout of him that by now is so bent out of shape that it can't even stand on its own two

feet. And you don't want to spend your entire life prop-
ping it up just to see its face.

So you broach the subject while sitting in the passenger's seat of your 1987 Chevy Nova, the beige fabric
hanging from the ceiling and framing the back seat like
stage curtains. You practically have to beg her for this
part of the story. You have to tell her that hearing the
excuses is finally getting harder than knowing the truth,
but you say it with the less practiced language of a second
grader whose face is always partially hidden between
two signature braids, and behind a giant pair of gold
Nickelodeon-brand glasses.

She tells you the stories about him that could be more
helpful than harmful. She tells you the ones where he's
smart or funny. The one about how they met. She tells
you that you have his nose. That you can draw because
of him. She gives you a version of him that you can see
yourself in. She saves the rest for later. Maybe some parts
are saved still, either forgotten or for what.

Alabama comes with humidity and hurricanes,
Confederate flags and college football, chicken-finger
chain restaurants and packs of chitterlings on sale two
for one at the big Winn-Dixie in Opelika, an aunt and
her husband and their kids who live forty minutes
away.

The water bugs scare your mother more than the
flags, the food, or the family.

In the beginning, you move from one apartment to the next to escape them. At least, that's what you gather from what you know about her and from what little you know about the world. Because you don't really know about money the same way you don't really know about fathers, you don't know how much you don't have. But you know that not having a lot is something you should probably learn to lie about if you don't want to get made fun of at school or at your aunt's house.

You know that you don't have a tape player in the Nova, so you can't choose your music. You think that maybe having money means the same as getting to choose. But until you have it—until you're rich from being a famous actor or a local doctor—you can only scan the FM stations in an endless search for something that isn't country or gospel or static, especially when there's nothing around you but tall trees and trailing kudzu. And because the options are limited, you have to know how your mother feels about every song—new or old. She keeps saying to you, "I like *talent*, Jill. Skill. That's why we mostly keep it on 104.1" (Jazz Flavors), whenever you forget and make the mistake of asking her why you can't listen to what everyone else is listening to.

You end up knowing more smooth jazz than any other kind of music, but you learn to lie about that, too.

She tries for you sometimes. Especially on Fridays after work, when she's sighing a little less from all that must be done to make do and due dates. She turns the station to 105.7 and waits for them to play the first song after a long commercial break.

And you wait, scared to even sing along to the first round of the chorus, because you know she won't last long. Even while basking in the warmth of an upcoming weekend, she can take only so much noise.

"Oh no. Uh-uh," she always ends up saying. "We can't do it, Jill. That music is made to destroy us. Seriously, Jill. They want you to think life is about money and partying and disrespecting women. Is that what you want life to be about?" Thankfully, she doesn't expect an answer. She just turns it back over to Jon Lucien or Gato Barbieri, and the sounds of Catalina Island roll in like waves from the speakers.

It's also why when your mother gets the black Saturn and the black Saturn has a tape player, you can listen to your Tevin Campbell or Brandy tapes. Everything else is for your room.

Anything by Immature is for your room.

The Shaggy "Boombastic" single cassette tape is for your room.

"That's why we got you the headphones, Jill," she says.

Even though it stops you from being as cool as some of the kids in your school who know all the words to all the popular songs, it also makes you want to know your own taste in everything. You want to know what you don't like and why, and how to explain why as well as she can, as passionately as she does. Developing language around liking things seems a lot less interesting, and you want to be interesting because you like being noticed— especially by adults.

Even by your grandparents, who by then have moved from California and into the house next door to your aunt and her husband and your cousins, and already started stirring the pot that promises to one day boil over, start a fire.

When your grandmother moves to Alabama and sees how close you are to your mother, she becomes particularly fixated on wedging her way in between. Intent on exposing your mother to you as someone you may not know as well as you think you do. She tells you that mothers and daughters shouldn't be best friends. She asks if your mother has been taking you to church. She asks you if you've spoken to your father. She calls him a mistake and you feel an unfamiliar urge to defend him, but only as a way of defending your mother.

They ask you how it starts, but they don't mean the creative writing lessons or the acting camps or the art classes your mother saved or shifted priorities to pay for, drove from work to pick you up from.

She would make dinner in your small apartment kitchen, still wearing her shoes and purse, singing the memory of the last song she had heard as she poured the required green vegetable from a can and into a one-quart pot with a missing lid.

Your mother has books everywhere. There are the thick green-and-black law books that she says are filled with things you better learn something about fast if you're black and broke in this country, like us.

You're glad she knows what's in them so she can know for both of you.

There are books displayed on the coffee table, crowded onto the rows of the bookcase you helped her put together—the one that arrived in a box at the door of the new house she buys in rural Alabama when you're seven and she's twenty-eight.

There are books on her pressed-wood bedside table with the beige tablecloth from Kmart, and yours with the navy blue one, too.

Every night before bed, she makes you scoot over and she reads to you. When you're younger, you choose *Berenstain Bears* or something from the *Just a Little Critter Collection*. You like the illustrations of the animals, the anthropomorphism, the idea of learning enough lessons to be considered good.

Sometimes you choose your favorite book about a black girl your age who *also* just has a mother. Or another about a black girl who doesn't appreciate the dress her mother sews her for a party because she wants the one her mother can't afford instead.

These lessons are harder, closer to home.

Later come the fiction books about enslaved children and girls who *also* don't hear from their fathers. There are illustrated versions of simplified Shakespearean plays that she got from Alabama Shakespeare Festival in Montgomery. You take day trips there on the weekends and random federal holidays, bring lunch from home and sit in the grass with the ducks. You walk around the museum and look at the pictures of the actors performing plays in the theater down the hall. The one that's so grand and dark and exciting that you almost can't stand it.

You tell your mother that you want to be an actress or a writer or work in a school cafeteria because you like pretend and books and food.

She starts letting you make your own lunch and she takes you to see *Malcolm X* at Carmike Cinema. When you get home, she shows you his autobiography in the bookcase, opens the cover and points, says, "Your name is right here. All the important books are already dedicated to you. They're yours."

She pulls *Invisible Man* from another row of books, "Especially this one," she says. "This one is going to be important to you one day."

She takes you to see *Panther*, buys the coffee-table book about the making of the movie, buys the soundtrack and plays it for months on end. You love it because it's the only time you can get away with listening to so much rap at once.

She takes you to see *Philadelphia*, too. Even though your head barely reaches the top of the reclining seat, you eat your gummy bears quietly and pay close attention.

When your teacher frowns, asks why your mother would take you to see "those kinds of movies," you understand what she means, so you tell your mother, and she writes your teacher a letter, volunteers to come talk to the class about black history and anything else your teacher is uncomfortable addressing.

"We're in Alabama, sweetie. We have to make sure they know who they're dealing with, don't we? She'll be fine. And if she's not nice to you on Monday, you tell me, and I'll have a talk with your principal. But she'll be nice. Trust me," she says, resolute.

You learn that whenever your mother is resolute, she's also psychic. When she's braiding your hair before school and she's telling you how she envisions your life as you grow older, you trust it. You head straight toward it like it's been predetermined by the stars.

One morning, after hundreds of slightly revised versions of your future predicted, she sees you going to college in California, writing books, changing the world, and you suddenly have a favorite.

When you're seven years old, you come out to her for the first time. You say it simply, because to you, it seems simple.

"I like girls."

Your mother says, "So, you think girls are pretty?"

And you say yes.

She tells you that it's okay to think that girls are pretty and asks if there's anything else you want to tell her. But there isn't, because first you need to figure out if you think girls are pretty or if it's something that might not be as okay.

So you wait.

She dates very little in front of you but tells you funny stories about men she has dates with sometimes, the ones who will never make it to meeting you. But then there is one who seems the readiest and the least threatening. The one who knows well enough to tell you that he's going to propose before he does it. Knows that you need to be there when it's in the idea stage.

You never actually grow to like him, but in the beginning he's okay enough, you guess. You're more curious about the new lifestyle that the marriage promises. With him around, there's suddenly more indulgence and excess. More eating out and more outfits, bigger vacations and a bigger house. Eventually, another room for another kid.

When you're nine years old, your mother picks you up from school and hands you an envelope. You open it quickly, excited to see a card, hoping to find money inside. But nothing falls out when you shake it, so you move on to reading it. This is how you find out that your mother is pregnant. A card congratulating you on getting to be a big sister.

But who the *fuck* ever asked you? Where was your warning, the request for your input when this was in the idea stage?

You rip up the card and scream at her about how much you hate it—all of it—and it feels good to try out rebellion. It's a new kind of release.

Your mother allows it for a while, tries to tell you how she understands, and you carry on, ranting and raving, just to see how far she'll let you go. Just so you know for the future when you need to rebel again.

When she finally says, "Okay, Jill. Now wait," in that way meant to remind you that's she's different, but not that kind of different, you find her limit.

You mark that spot.

Your mother lets you choose his middle name. "Christian Slater" is one of the coolest names you've heard by the time you're nine years old, so Christian it is. Your brother arrives in July 1996, just like he was always meant to.

Becoming his sister is one of the most important things you ever become.

In a way it all starts when you begin to perform being funny in public and in public school, because it's important to you that you be impressive, do your part, hold up your end of the bargain you were always making with your mother.

It was as if the two of you were always silently promising "You do your best by me and I do my best by you, got it?"

But then doing your best gets complicated because all your crushes are (still) on girls. And doing your best by her begins to mean lying, but you never want to be the one who doesn't make good on your promise.

It's not that you think your mother will have a big reaction or take badly to the news. It's more that you don't want to alter her expectations for what your life will be. You don't want to surprise her.

In school, you can't quite figure out how to be both yourself and everyone else, too. Get what you want and get what adults want for you, too. So you stop trying.

You can't explain why your mother seems relieved when you start caring less about grades and more about figuring out what you believe in, how those beliefs will shape your life. She shows up to parent-teacher conferences, obviously excited to tell them how much she doesn't give a fuck what they think of her child, but in the language of a woman with a lot of debt from law school and a low-paying nonprofit job. Her sentences are short and to the point. She returns all questions with questions. She rushes them through their answers.

She's on her lunch break. What else?

"Maybe you're the problem," she says, straightening her blazer, "Maybe it's not Jill at all. Maybe it's your class."

She seems way more excited to defend you than she ever did to see your outstanding report card. You change schools—and teachers—a lot. She is almost never satisfied with what the school system or the after-school program or the world has to offer you. She wants everything to be better than it is, as good as she thinks both you and your brother are.

In high school, you do nothing but start drama and join the club, because by now you care only about world peace and the girls you have crushes on, the ones you write about in your diary. Three or more times a week, you update a nonexistent reader on how many words each crush has said to you that week, desperate to tell someone who gets it.

You wear your giant political buttons—the ones you pick up at protests and political potlucks organized by the mostly white and performatively multicultural Unitarian church—pinned through the rough, multicolored fabric of one of your many Baja jackets. It's probably the jackets and the tie-dye T-shirts (the ones your mom's friend from Oakland taught you to make when she visited for a week over the summer) and all the hemp jewelry that earn you the title of "Most Wanted by the Fashion Police" in your unofficial senior poll. But you don't mind. In fact, the title is the point.

You spend most of the day hanging out in the nooks and crannies of your school, talking shit with your friends and avoiding class. But you never miss your curfew at home once. You still help with your brother and you still clean your room after only two asks from your mother. You would still rather be at home, talking about the world, than in the world, talking about home.

Even if it turns out that your stepfather is more threatening than he originally advertised.

He's brought with him a world of screaming and threats and cops and sudden change.

You want to believe in good and bad because you believe you're good. But your stepfather makes it impossible. You have to learn how to live with a character you wish you could understand more. You want to know what he thinks he's defending himself against. You want him to make sense. But he doesn't want to.

So you do the work of forcing yourself to see him as complicated. You come up with hundreds of different explanations for him. Make him into a hundred different people. Learn to believe that you like some of them as a way of making life easier.

Becoming someone who would eventually gain a moment of micro-fame on social media might have started when your mother learns of a mismatched caravan of old southern activists who are heading up to D.C. to protest the war on Iraq. She says to you, "I know you have school, but let's be honest, you're not doing anything there. And this is school, too. So you should go. I think it'll be good for you." And you know that she must be worried more about your restlessness than about her paranoia to even suggest it.

You go and going changes your whole fucking life.

The first leg of the trip is from the church to Huntsville, where you will join the people who have the van big enough for everybody. You drive there after school with a British woman who teaches English at Auburn, and that night you both stay at Steve and Mary's house. It's a predictable old bungalow with rainbow afghans draped across every piece of aged furniture and a record collection so massive that its stacks have spilled into the unlit fireplace and stayed long enough to gather dust.

You sleep in their thirteen-year-old daughter's extra bed, and all night long she tries to talk to you about bands you've heard of but don't want to talk about, and her mean friends from school, and what you like to do for fun.

In the morning, you are more ready for the road than ever.

The caravan of eight picks up the last person in Knoxville. Someone your age. He has a lime-green mohawk and tells you before you can ask that he's an anarchist. You have to pretend you know what that is, because asking questions is still something that embarrasses you, and because you have a feeling that he likes to give a long answer to a short question.

You have Indian food for the first time in Virginia and stay awake to keep Steve company as you finish the drive into D.C. You sleep in a hotel room with eight other people who, like you, think they have all their own ideas. In that moment, your ideas agree and it's a massive relief—the first moment of relief from shared ideas that you ever have.

You agree that you want peace on earth, equal rights for all, an end to corporate corruption. You want people to invest in love and freedom and hope instead of domination and greed. You don't know if you disagree on how to get there, because you don't talk very much about how to get there. Only where you need to go.

You look around the room and feel alone with yourself in a way that you've never felt before. It's not lonely. Just new.

The next morning, you lose yourself in a crowd of protest signs and alternative aesthetics, and it feels so good you want to cry. You walk the streets of D.C. and try out being this version of yourself that you think just might be your entire self forever, in person.

When you get back home, you tell your mother all about it even though you've had to call her at every stop you've made, there and back. You know it must cost a fortune because you aren't calling after 9 P.M. or on a weekend, and no one you know is really texting yet because it's way too expensive.

Your mother tells you that you seem older, and it's still your favorite compliment to have received.

When you get back to school, your science teacher, who doesn't like you—who knows you're not taking anything seriously—asks where you were and why she should let you do the makeup assignments. You don't really care to do them, so you tell her the truth. That you went to D.C. to protest the war because your mom says it's just as important as school.

She smiles at you like she's seeing you for the very first time, grabs you by your shoulders like a coach, cheers.

"That's *it*! That's the real stuff, Jill!"

And this time you smile, because you're seeing something about her for the very first time, too.

She allows you to do the assignments you missed and never unsees you again. So you finish out the rest of her class by taking it seriously. This is the kind of bargain that you know and respect, so it's easy to honor it.

One weekend, your mother shows you the undergraduate catalog from the weird school in San Francisco where she went for law school and you walked across the stage with her at graduation. She says that it's for people like you and you don't know which "like you" she means, but you know she's telling you to *run*.

To go be yourself somewhere farther away, for longer.

New College asks for transcripts but the admissions office informs you that good grades are the very least of what they want from you—which is good, because you don't have any good grades to give them. Instead, they require a five-page answer to the question "How do you plan to change the world?"

Happy to finally be asked, you finish it in an afternoon, write about how you will use your acting and your writing as tools. People need to be *convinced*. The people trying to change the world for the better need to make what we believe in seem like the only option, the only solution. A real no-brainer.

Don't you have to sell it if you want other people to buy it? Don't you have to make them need it?

And when they send you your acceptance letter and you know that you're leaving Auburn, Alabama, for San Francisco, California, in the fall of 2004, you're too overwhelmed to be excited.

Also, there's a girl that you found on the internet. You talk to her every night on the phone for hours, and lying to your mother makes your body feel less hospitable, your stomach less accepting of its contents. So when she finds you crying on your bed with the door closed, your first instinct is to eject something vital.

"What's going on?" she asks in that voice that means you better tell her before she gets too worried.

This time it's hard. You recognize the tone and what she expects, but this time you can't. You don't know how to make it come out of your mouth.

"Jill."

It's a warning.

"l can't tell you," you say with your head between your knees.

"Did someone hurt you? Are you pregnant? Wait, Jill, are you on drugs?"

"No, none of those things."

"Is it about a boy?" she asks.

Instead of the vomit you were anticipating, the truth makes its way from your gut and up through your lips and you say, "It'll never be about a boy."

And even in the moment you think to yourself, "What kind of fucking Lifetime movie, *The Truth About Jane* shit is this?" and you wish that there was someone to watch this happen, to laugh at the parts that aren't funny to you just yet but will be later.

"You like girls?" she asks, looking at you through narrowed eyes.

"Yes! Yes, I like girls."

She nods for a moment, then promptly slams your door, manages to shock you even more than you've shocked yourself. Because no, you never planned on telling her, for reasons you can no longer remember, but still, you thought that maybe . . .

But then you hear her footsteps making their way back to your room. She swings the door open and walks over to you and it happens too quickly for you to even consider the options for what might happen.

"Jill, I thought something was actually wrong. I thought it was something *bad*."

She's mad that you would scare her, and you tell her that you were scared, too. She gets yet another reason to demand more from the world on behalf of her kids, and reasons were the last things she needed.

When she drops you off at the airport in the fall, waves as you make your way toward the security line, she's the saddest she's ever let herself be in front of you.

It's an affirmation you never knew you needed.

*

NEW COLLEGE SCARES the shit out of you because something feels eerily the same.

You thought you'd finally be an insider. For once, a part of a welcoming majority, united by an overwhelming desire to right the wrongs of greedy white men in suits, fight the good fight.

But in a school full mostly of white people with radical philosophies and acid-birthed solutions for someone else's problems, you feel more outside of a culture than you've ever felt, the only one of everything, always raising your hand to point out what's missing from the conversation, but also being enough of it for them to feel like it's there.

Eventually, you start taking pleasure in interrupting their theories with personal experiences and points of reference that they couldn't know or disprove. Being outside becomes useful. Being the only one with a first-hand account makes you an indisputable source. An expert.

You get used to that feeling.

You take a class called Writing Well I and have a writing teacher (New College doesn't call them professors) who gives you a B on your first essay. And as someone who has barely graduated from high school out of an utter lack of interest, you can't explain why you care. Why it's suddenly not good enough.

But also, you can. Because you want to be the winner this time. Now that it's *your* stuff, you want to be good at it.

For the next essay, you write about your roommate at Ansonia Abby—the student housing facility you are living in since New College doesn't have dorms. All the students from the fashion and language schools live there, too, making for the kind of diversity that no one means.

Your roommate is from Japan and she is in San Francisco to learn English. She shows you pictures of her boyfriend, brings you bananas from the cafeteria when you decide to sleep in. She is neat and considerate, and so are you. You say "Good morning!" to each other every morning and "Good night!" to each other every evening after she kindly asks you if you're also ready to turn the lights off. Even if you aren't, you say yes and go to bed, too.

One time she asks if you will help her review for a test, and it's the most you ever talk. The next day, she leaves a piece of chocolate cake she bought from the bakery down the street on your dresser, along with a thank-you note.

In the essay you describe the bathroom you share, the hair products, the clippers you use to shave your head, her Herbal Essences rose-scented shampoo with directions that you can't understand. She's in San Francisco to learn English and you're in San Francisco to learn double-talk.

You get an A on the essay, and your teacher (whom you call by her first name) pulls you aside to tell you how much she's looking forward to reading your weekly assignments.

You're taking an experimental performance-art class, a class on Freud in the media. You're also taking a class on revolutionary African literature, but you lose interest after your teacher tells you how much he paid for his Italian leather shoes. How he wouldn't be caught dead wearing anything else.

But that's not the only reason.

There's a tension between the two of you that you can't name. A tension that you've never felt before with another black person—especially a black person at New College. In fact, you are all overly friendly with each other, winking and shrugging at each other across the room of white actors and activists.

When you ask questions, he smirks.

When you answer questions, he laughs before he responds.

When you tell him that your final project will be on Indigenous Australian culture, he says, "Of course it will be."

Like you're obvious to him. Predictable.

You never completely diagnose it, but it doesn't even matter. Because suddenly, you care about nothing but Writing Well I and the weekly essays you're assigned. You write each one to the very fullest of your ability. You can't think of another time you've cared like this or when it's meant so much. But she can tell that it does, so she writes you detailed notes all throughout the paragraphs, full-page notes on the back of the last page. She notices almost everything you do on purpose and tells you when it works.

You fall in love with what you can do with an essay. The contradictions you can name without implicating yourself in any of them, the way you get to control the narrative. You learn a new way to sell something.

The final exam—a timed personal essay on anything you want—was exactly how you desired to end the semester. You write and write and you do it joyfully. For fun.

That's why at the end of the year, when everyone who showed up to even half of the once-a-week classes— sometimes literally with a pet macaw on their shoulder or a banjo instead of a book—gets an A, you want to burn the entire building to the ground.

No one would think that it starts when you confront your teacher in the café because you don't know how to stop being angry without an answer.

"Jill, you wrote great essays in this class. But everyone was trying their best. It wouldn't be fair to give you the highest grade if everyone was trying their best. Don't you want them to feel encouraged?"

It'll be a full decade before you write another personal essay, and you never write to the best of your ability at New College again. You don't have to. You get As with minimal effort so that no one feels like they're re-creating the patriarchy.

You are taught by alternative capitalists, egalitarian egomaniacs, and old-school hippiecrites with time to spare now that some time has passed. Many of them are desperate for the good old days when their gripes were the most progressive, frustrated to hear the language change without them. Angry that they could get something wrong now and quickly become the enemy of the later generations of themselves.

And even though your teachers were educated at Ivy Leagues and are the children of famous writers and actresses, agents and politicians, they have chosen to come teach you the lessons of their heroic half-rebellion. Pass on their politics for the sake of their own personal preservation. They believe that your belief in them and what they believe is what makes you smart. So the trying doesn't quite matter.

They needed Harvard, but somehow you only need them.

And everyone who needs them should feel encouraged.

After you leave the school and return, and even after you leave again and it closes its doors for good—without immediately repaying money owed to staff and students or honoring the agreements of its own ethical framework and without a real apology for its incongruous actions—the obsession with spotting anyone and everything that isn't who or what it claims to be, that doesn't live in complete agreement with who and what it says it is, intensifies. It started within your own family, for your own protection.

You don't want to get burned again. Not even by yourself.

So you begin to see your own contradictions as weakness, develop a fear of finding out that you're not who you think you are and an additional fear of being called out for it by other people.

Maybe it starts with fear.

*

YOU'RE IN YOUR midtwenties when you begin facilitating "cultural competency" trainings with your mother for nonprofit organizations all over the California Bay Area. She's the one with the real experience. You've spent most of your twenties working odd jobs and signing on to message boards to earn participation credit for online classes, trying to avoid being a contradiction by not being much of anything at all.

But you have a queer identity and a generational perspective that lengthen the list of training topics and widen your potential reach in a room. So she mentors you, teaches you everything she knows about nonprofits. She teaches you about mission and vision statements. She teaches you about grants and how they fund programming. She teaches you about all the different levels of staff and what they do. She also gives you tips on public speaking, teaches you social service lingo, shorthand.

Your mother is always finding new clients to train and new trainings to give (Culture & Media, Boundaries, Family Advocacy Parts I & II, Queer Advocacy Parts I & II, Conflict Resolution, Home-Visiting Basics, Strategic Planning, Organizational Storytelling & Timelining, Outreach & Engagement Parts I & II, Restorative Justice, Team Building) because she's friendly and relentless, and so you're always throwing on your Banana Republic sweater and your "serious pants" and getting in the passenger's side of your Hyundai Tucson, inching down the congested freeways of progress, surrounded by Blizzard Pearl, Blue Ribbon or Barcelona Red Metallic Priuses (diversity) with Hillary '08 and Obama '12 bumper stickers (inclusion), headed to some training, somewhere.

In the beginning, you're just along for the ride, unconvinced that a training can actually change anything. But all the nonprofit organizations that enlist your services are receiving grant money for working with adopted and fostered children and the stakes are too high.

If you don't take every question from the foster parent who wants to know if she can let a queer child sleep in the same room as the other kids she's fostering, and if you don't answer them in a way that doesn't shame her into shutting down, there's a child who suffers for your apathy, your waste of an opportunity with a person who's asking a hard but seemingly genuine question—the system they're in will impact them whether you believe in its intentions or not.

Yeah, it's all fucked. But you're in the front of a room with twenty pairs of eyes on you and the clock moves slowly. So you might as well try.

You better try.

Together, as the disarmingly weird, multigenerational comedic duo, you and your mother become a team like no other. And it works.

Instead of implicating themselves in the experiences of their token diversity employees, nonprofits hire the two of you as the insider outsiders (or the outsider insiders?) who can affirm and suggest from an impossible distance, take no one's side but the children's. You're there to reinforce the organizational vision, hold management accountable, and strengthen everyone's comfort in working through new or "culturally challenging" interactions with coworkers and clients.

But everyone wants something different from you. The social workers want you to put their supervisor on the spot at least once, make them have to admit to something they've done wrong. Like made an assumption about a client's racial background in a weekly meeting or crossed a boundary with a supervisee during an all-staff training. You know we've done our job when a social worker smirks, raises an eyebrow, hides a laugh, turns to a coworker, and shares a secret smile.

The clinical supervisors want to hear that change starts at the very top. That they're trying to get the job done with limited time and resources and they don't feel heard or supported by the regional director. You know what would also be helpful? A script for how to handle a variety of cross-cultural incidents and staff complaints. They want to know what they can say and what they can't. They want one size to fit all as long as it makes the workday shorter.

The regional director wants the training to check off a few boxes for the old grants and even more for the new ones. They want to hear that they are more proactive and culturally aware than other regional directors. They think it might be helpful to review the mission and vision of the organization, make sure they are culturally current so that they can update them on the website.

You both do it until you can't anymore. Until you don't know what you're saying or why you're saying it. Until your favorite organization—the one that seems most sincere in its efforts, most connected to the work and the clients—closes its doors for lack of funding while organizations that exist only to chase grants thrive.

Until people you train begin to get sick and, without health coverage, die.

Until one of the organizations wins all the grants and expands into communities it knows nothing about. Suddenly it can afford to hire you for every type of training you've got, one at every location, and you can't say no.

Until you think of your mother saying, "But what is the social services incentive to ever solve the problem? They'd put themselves right out of a job," and you can't stop thinking about it.

Until you ask the group with all the money a question, "What do white people offer in a cultural exchange?" and the white queer woman who is a director gets defensive, doesn't understand that it's a trick question designed to make white people admit that they have culture.

"You're saying white people have nothing to offer?" she asks incredulously.

"No," you respond, meaning it. "I'm asking what white people offer—culturally—in an exchange with someone of another culture. When we discussed diversity, people talked about all the language and yummy food and rich traditions people bring into the office and how that benefits the overall culture of the office. Alma asked if tradition is always beneficial, and as a room, we agreed that it's not. Just now, Sam was sharing some of the things he had learned from his travels through Asia and how they had impacted his life. I asked if he felt like he had offered something in exchange for what he learned—which we agreed doesn't always happen. Then

Natalie asked if that kind of exchange should always happen."

"Right. And then you asked what white people offer in return for what they get. And I'd have to say *a lot*," she says, laughs, leaning back in her chair, crossing her arms.

"Great, perfect. Did you want to share some of what came up for you or should we turn it back ov—"

"I'll share. Infrastructure, resources, educational opportunities . . . *um* . . . in some cases, actual money, aid. I know a lot of smart white people who have dedicated their lives to scientific research, public health, helping people. Generous people. Um, teachers."

"And you feel like those things are all cultural? And part of white culture, specifically?"

"What is *white culture*? Why is that so broad?"

"Well, that's what I'm asking. That's what we're trying to figure out."

"I think they're part of American culture, and white culture gave you America. A place where we're allowed to have this training."

You're in shock because she's supposed to think it, sure, but never say it in public. At work. That's not how the script goes. And because she's already gone too far, she keeps going still and ends up saying how proud she is to live somewhere where people care about each other, and other people should be proud, too—even if it's fucked up sometimes for people like her or "you." You don't know which part of you she's talking about. The parts you share or the parts you don't.

Most people disengage, look down at their phones or their laps or a handout. The one black employee starts mumbling under her breath, "Fuck this shit," and the people she works with start to stare at her, and your mother tries to save it by suggesting everyone take a break, come back and move on to a small-group activity. But the room has changed. And you realize that when the training is over, you and your mother will leave and the time some director told you she gave you America will be nothing more than an anecdote, a memory from your training days. Something you remind each other of when you want to get mad for fun.

You don't work there. The stakes aren't as high.

You never return to that office. When you run into the director at the other offices in Oakland or in trainings for upper management, you exchange smiles and leave it at that.

After a few years, the trainings are more for the organizations that like you and want to see you back again, doing something. *Anything.* So there are always new trainings. New topics. Part fours and fives of old trainings.

But Barack is still president. Federally recognized gay marriage is right around the corner. Police shootings are still mostly local news. People need only so much cultural competence when everything is going so well.

Jillisblack and the sub-demographic micro-fame start when you and your mother visit your brother at school in Olympia, Washington, and fall in love with it. The trees, the coffee, the air. The parks and all the available parking. Mount Rainier. You feel like you can breathe. Like there's space for your breath.

The last day of your trip, you sit together at a coffee shop downtown, right in front of the window. You tell her that you're dreading going home. That it feels like you're leaving a new one.

"I agree," she says, casually sipping her coffee like she hasn't already made up her mind. "Maybe we should try it."

A few months later, you do.

In Olympia, your mother is overqualified for every position she goes out for and you get hired only because you're black but also queer.

Olympia does queer. Black is out of its wheelhouse.

So you work as a program coordinator at a small nonprofit for queer youth. Then you leave to go work for a large nonprofit, where you're paid to "do" diversity and inclusion. When they hire you, they tell you that it was a plus that you are black, but also your queerness allows you to do more trainings in the community—which gave you an advantage over the other person they were considering for the position.

You don't actually know how to do anything they're asking you to do besides train, but you know how to interview for it. And you'll do whatever you need to do, sell whatever part of yourself the job requires, because there's rent and groceries and cell phone plans.

You need your cell phone plan.

You're surrounded by trees and coffee and air, but also an impenetrable level of whiteness. And yes, it speaks to you in the grocery store, makes room for you on the trails. Asks you how long you've been vegan and gives you a high five. Sends its "kiddos and doggos" over to say hello to you at the park. It's mostly friendly and so are you.

But at the time, it's also lonely. You feel like a permanent exception, a guest. Forever being asked what event you're in town for or what your major is at Evergreen. You run into people you've met before who either seem scared to say they remember meeting you or genuinely don't.

Because you're lonely, you're on Instagram more than ever. You get high every night and follow everyone that you wish you could hang out with in real life. Sometimes they follow you back. The more followers you gain, the more likely they are to follow back. And the people you follow, follow each other.

For once, you're not the only version of anything that you are.

These strangers you share identities and interests and musical taste and exes and politics and hairstyles with become your community.

A chosen community of people like you from all over the globe. People who finally make you feel like the majority. People who are either in agreement with you or quickly unfollowed, replaced, forgotten about. People you've never met but feel like you already know.

You begin to post a few times a week.

This is how it starts.

[Dear Dad]

Because I found you nowhere
I choose to find you elsewhere
In men whose layers
Have kept me warm in the absence of your apology.
I will sew a father-shaped quilt
Out of the fabric of these better men
And when it's time
I will pass it down.

Love,
Your Daughter

—*Jillisblack*, June 2017

A FRIEND OF MEN

As always, I am assigned the middle seat on a flight to New York. By the time I find my row, there is already a woman fast asleep in the window seat. Her face is tucked into her antecubital space, and her body is folded into its very smallest shape so as not to disturb anyone. I sit down in the middle seat—24B—between her and the empty seat, and wait. I want to see who else is coming before making a decision about how I will best fit.

When I see him walk up the aisle—early forties, white enough, maybe divorced or divorcing, maybe someone's father—I know it will be him. He's wearing a blue-checkered button-down shirt, relaxed-fit weekend khakis, silver-rimmed glasses on a squarish face. I can't help but notice that he's just a little bit shorter than me, a little bit bald on the top.

I know I'm not supposed to notice all the little bits, because that means I'm looking too closely.

At first, we barely make eye contact, choosing to keep our smiles tight, polite, and fleeting. He slides his smart black carry-on into the overhead bin, points at his seat. My right elbow leaves the armrest, my right thigh slides farther center. My entire body shifts left, closer to the folded woman. I make more room for him than I leave for myself, and when he sits, he stretches out into every corner of it because it's there.

"Hi," I say, dropping my voice, using my countertenor.

He, unsuspecting to the point of insult, stares at me blankly, then says, "Oh, hello."

There is silence for a while, and the occasional apology for any unexpected touching of shoulders, elbows, knees. Then the apologizing grows too tedious and the unexpected touching too expected, so what remains is the silence. As we reach a cruising altitude and the "fasten seat belt" light fades, I turn to him and say, "Do you want to do your own thing, or should we have a conversation?"

He laughs, surprised. Then he shrugs a *Why not?*, turns his body toward me.

"How do we start?" he asks.

*

*

MY MOTHER STILL tells the story, asks if I remember Michael and the preschool teacher who would tell her every day that I was the only one who could calm him, bring him back down to earth.

He is one of my earliest memories. Not of another person, but of myself.

He had all the attention, always kicking and screaming, upset and inconsolable. On the rare occasion that he was allowed to be in a room with the rest of us, it was only a matter of time before he'd have to be picked up and taken out, a bright red emergency. I remember being relieved when the tantrum would finally happen and I could stop waiting for it.

I couldn't figure out why there were boys in the class who could sit still, color, take naps, play games, and make friends, and then there was Michael, who couldn't do any of those things. What was *he*?

Because the other boys were the majority, they weren't all that interesting. Why learn more about them if they already made sense? If their alikeness was already forming a pattern?

Why not solve the difference of Michael and actually get somewhere? Figure out if I was more like the boys who could sit still or if I was more like him?

I already knew I didn't seem like the other girls. But I didn't know why that difference didn't make me an emergency like Michael.

I know there are a number of reasons why Michael was prone to make a scene. But back then, with few points of reference or ways to name what I saw, I found him to be absolutely fascinating. I wanted to understand what I sensed: that he was a small part of a much larger story about carrying out contrary impulses.

I knew I couldn't scream or make a scene like Michael could. But I wanted to know *how* I knew. More than that, I wanted to know why I didn't *want* to scream or make a scene like he did. Why, to me, it felt out of the realm of possibility, and how he knew he *could* do those things in the first place. How he let himself do them.

How I didn't.

I wanted to understand that gap between.

I remember approaching him, sitting with him in the corner, saying nothing. I remember doing it day after day, until one day I started asking him questions—at least the questions I had learned so far to ask (maybe thirty or so, but it was enough)—and handing him toys to try. I remember him trying to answer through the lingering tremors of his last bout, his skin tight from the layers of dried tears.

I also remember the praise I got for my ability to subdue him with my focused attention and how it felt—how powerful I felt even though I didn't yet know the word or my own desire for it. Michael got attention for his outbursts, and I got attention for soothing Michael. Eventually, he sought me out whenever he was upset, exploded even bigger when I wasn't around to ground him with questions about himself.

Michael was the first boy I ever felt responsible for, ever took on as a way of trying to be more myself.

Mutualism: A form of symbiosis that is characterized by both species benefiting from the association.
Parasitism: One organism benefits while causing the other harm.
Commensalism: One organism benefits while the other is unaffected.

After Michael, there was Samuel. I was visiting with my grandparents in Oakland for a couple of months, going to their church down the hill. Samuel was in my Sunday school class. I would go over to his house and marvel at his toys, take the opportunity to play with them without my grandmother watching carefully for signs of what I might be or want.

His toys were hard metal and thick plastic, ramp and pulley, construction and demolition, law and order, fast and flame. On his bedroom floor was a giant activity rug that looked like a town. There were winding roads and stoplights, municipal buildings and trees.

I loved it. I loved anything that imitated real (adult) life.

I liked dolls, too. One time I brought them to Samuel's house, spread them out on that rug and told him he could choose the ones he wanted. He laughed like I was stupid, told me that dolls were for girls, and so I put them away.

We spent the next three hours racing Matchbox cars in circles.

I could do what he did *with him* when it was just the two of us, but he could never do what I did, with or without me, *ever*. No one could see him do it. Not even himself.

Later there would be more and more of these friendships, all made out of the same threads.

There was John the Freshman, whom I am assigned to sit next to when I have to retake physical science my sophomore year of high school. He's the quarterback of the JV football team. Wears camo, jeans with cowboy boots, and—on game day—his blue-and-white jersey. The class sits in three lines of paired desks. I sit next to him and his camo in my tie-dye shirts and antiwar buttons. We don't talk until one day we do, and then we don't stop talking for the rest of the semester, nearly obsessed with our own novelty.

I'm writing a story about a girl who falls in love with a boy she meets in rehab, and every day John the Freshman reads my new pages and gives me feedback. The one time I come to class without anything new, he shakes his head at me, lays the guilt on thick, "This is no good, Busby. I need to know what happens."

When the teaching assistant tries to move us to quiet the constant talking, we're both so genuinely distraught and loud about it that by the end of the week, he's moved us back and warns us that we'll have to be more quiet, less disruptive.

But then John starts dating Jenna, the junior varsity cheerleader from my debate class. They're a hometown tradition, and I'm disappointed that he's finally stopped contradicting himself in such an obvious way.

It's so fucking boring.

After the end of the semester, we never speak again, and years later I find out that he joined the navy, proposed to Jenna in New York, married her back home in front of all their classmates, who also know how to sit still, color, take naps, play games, and make friends.

Even when the boys were called my "boyfriends," they were really just friends. I would choose a favorite, flatter him with my sudden interest, ask him to be my boyfriend. Having a boyfriend meant freedom from being asked why I didn't have a boyfriend, so I was hardly ever without one if I could help it.

Aggressive mimicry: A form of similarity in which a predator or parasite gains an advantage by its resemblance to a third party.

By junior year, there were other things that influenced the way I made my friends. So there was Kahlil. He was secretly gay like me. It was almost all we talked about because it was the one thing we couldn't talk about with anyone else. We would leave debate class to go do "research" and instead escape to the deepest, darkest corner of the library to update each other on everything new that had happened with the people we had crushes on. We would analyze the interactions or lack thereof and decide what we were going to do about it—which, by the way, was absolutely nothing.

We had in common this circumspection, this hesitation.

I was scared of not being liked and possibly being killed for *who* I liked. He was scared of God's wrath and even more scared of his mother's.

*
*

THE WOMAN IN seat 24A has yet to move a muscle.

The man next to me is opening a package of cookies.

I ask him if he lives in New York.

He asks me if I live in New York.

I ask him if he likes living in New York.

He asks me if I live alone.

I tell him that I'm married.

He asks me how long I've been with my husband.

He nods, recovers quickly enough, says, "Oh, I see."

He asks me how long I've been with my wife.

He asks me if I've only ever been with women, stumbles over it.

I ask him if he's only ever been with women.

He laughs nervously. "Yes, yes, yes!"

I don't laugh.

"It's a real question," I say.

He stops laughing. "Yes. Yes, I understand."

A flight attendant announces that they will now be starting their complimentary food and beverage service.

He takes out his wallet.

Tells me he's going to get a beer.

Asks if he can buy me a drink.

I shake my head.

Say thank you.

"But thank you," I say.

I ask where he's from.

I ask if he misses Vienna.

He asks where I'm from.

He asks which one feels more like home.

He tells me he's never been to Alabama.

I tell him it's not for everyone.

He says nothing ever is and I agree.

I ask how long he can stay in New York.

He tells me his job is moving him to Geneva next week, and as he says it, he breathes a sigh of relief. "There are trees everywhere in Geneva. And I will have time to see them. I am excited, yes."

I ask him what he does for work.

I ask him if he likes it.

I ask him what else he does.

"I want to retire in five years and study baking, pastries. Then I want to open a dessert shop."

He asks me what else I do.

I tell him that I'm working on a book proposal.

He asks me what the book will be about.

"No matter what I say it's about, it's actually about me being scared. Of other people, of the internet, of trying too hard. Or it's about power. How we make ourselves feel powerful when we don't feel empowered."

> **Batesian mimicry:** A form of biological resemblance in which a noxious, or dangerous, organism (the model), equipped with a warning system such as conspicuous coloration, is mimicked by a harmless organism (the mimic).

He nods, doesn't say anything, stretches his legs, sips his beer.

"I took an edible," I tell him for no reason.

"Ah, good for you. I just do alcohol."

He reaches for the *Sky* mag, flips through the pages back to front, stretches his legs, sips his beer.

Then he asks, "Do you feel like you have power?"

"Over myself—so yes. Over anyone else, no. But I try anyway."

He looks at me like, *Say more.*

"It's hard. I feel most powerful when I feel like I'm being myself. But I don't even try to be myself in public. Like, the idea of going out into the world as just Jill scares the shit out of me. So I'm always a little bit in character. And that character feels more powerful than I do."

He nods, smiles.

"I'm not sure that other people often feel like themselves either—even these people that we're supposed to think are so powerful," he says.

"Do you feel like you have power?" I ask.

He thinks.

"Well, I don't know. In this country and where I come from, too, I am certainly given a lot of power."

"Do you have power that you didn't get from someone else?"

"Yes, sure. But I'm talking about power in the . . ."

"In the society?"

"Yes, in society."

"In society I have power that I get from other people, too."

He looks at me like he can't tell if I'm serious.

He asks, "What is your character like?"

I laugh. "Funny. Dry, you know. Unimpressed. Kind of . . . removed. Unemotional. Hard to know. She likes to dominate conversations because she likes to convince people of how smart she is. How she can't be tricked."

"Are you sure she's not just you?"

"Of course not."

We laugh.

The flight attendant interrupts us with the offer of coffee or water.

"Coffee," I say.

"Coffee," he says.

"Black," I say.

"Black," he says.

The steam dances—coffee too hot to drink—and we sit in a preferred discomfort, a learned compromise.

When the plane lands and the flight is over, we exchange email addresses, hug at the arrivals gate.

"I hope you do well with your book," he says.

"I'm going to write about you."

"I don't believe you."

"You'll believe it when it's true."

"Maybe not even then."

"Oh, *there's* your real power!" I say, and we both laugh.

Leave it.

*
*
*

THREE HOURS AFTER I land in New York, I find myself at a trendy restaurant with a rooftop bar with a group of a certain kind of friend.

Jillisblack makes different kinds of friends than I can. So I am now friends with the kind of men I couldn't have met without her. The kind who knew me as her, first, and think they are getting to know her better whenever I show up as myself, instead.

They wanted the outdoor seating, and the table is too small for all of us. It's also the only one available, so we try to make it work. I sit wedged between Shawn and Louis, their after-work biceps wide and imposing inside summer-tight short sleeves. There's also Jared and the two Kyles and Marcus. We are all black, a few of us queer, but I am the only woman at the table. And I notice because I have learned to notice something I am when I am the only one of it.

Shawn was the first friend, and still my favorite. Successful, late thirties, charismatic, and flirtatious, an underdog done good, a black man in a suit on Monday and a jersey on Saturday, good-looking to enough people that it had become a relevant identity, all dressed up as himself with somewhere else to be.

He knows it. He does himself as an act. On purpose.

I like the on-purpose of him and he likes that I've noticed what's on-purpose about him, so we're friends.

"Jill, you still vegan?"

"Always."

"Alright, well, look. I'm sorry you can't eat any of this good-ass food. Kyle, are you getting wings, man?"

"Yeah, man. And probably, like, let me see . . . probably the plantains. I really don't need all that shit, though, man. I'm in Thailand next week, but I'm thinking of doing a juice cleanse as soon as I get back."

He caresses his torso, reassures himself.

"Oh yeah? My homie—you know Calvin?"

"Yeah, I know Calvin. That's the dude who's got the movie coming out, right?"

"Yeah, the documentary. He's a director."

"Yeah, Calvin. I know Calvin. He's a cool dude."

"Yeah, Calvin's a cool dude."

A table leaves, another is seated, the waitress is back with waters, drinks, ready to take our order. She answers all the questions, substitutes all the sides, says, "Yes, we can do that," smiles, nods, turns, smiles again.

"Jill, you saw *Homecoming*?" Kyle asks.

"The Beyoncé thing?" Marcus asks.

"No, it's not for me," I say, and brace myself for the . . .

"Is that even allowed?" the other Kyle asks, smiling, amused.

"Not at every table, no," I say.

"Why isn't it for you?"

"I'm just not a Beyoncé fan."

"I'm about to call every black woman I know and tell on you. That's what I'm about to do."

Laughter.

"Do it," I say, "so I can tell on you to every black woman you know, too."

Shawn looks at me, wants the real answer. "You don't think she's important?"

"Everyone's important," I say.

He waves his hands, rushing me to it. "No, for real."

"So you don't think she's a feminist, huh?" Louis asks.

"I'm more concerned that I can't say I'm not a fan without inviting that question. Years ago, when I could say that I wasn't a fan without inviting that question, *that's* when I was kind of a fan," I say, laughing.

"Are *you* a feminist?" Shawn asks.

"Are *you*?"

"I think men need to reevaluate our masculinity, for sure. And I think women are incredible. I think they're smart and capable and strong, and I think we, as men, need to be listening to y'all right now. I think rape culture is out of control, so . . . yeah. I'd say I'm a feminist. I'm not perfect, but I'm trying to learn how to be a better man."

"A better man or a better feminist?" I ask, sipping my water.

"I mean, shit. Both, I guess. Same thing, right?"

Later, after he declares himself a feminist who wants to be a better man, I watch Shawn walk by a woman at the bar, touch her, rest a hand on the small of her back, turn her around, lean in. I watch him tell her that she's beautiful. I watch the hand not move.

I wait.

I ask myself, "How does this work?"

I watch him begin a conversation with her. There is talking and smiling and I don't get it. What does this mean? Do I not understand something about straightness?

What if she and I don't agree about what a woman should want done to her body? Do I not get to say what a woman should want done to her body? Is attempting to do that inherently antifeminist?

Whose agenda wins here—mine or hers? What happens when we don't agree? Do I go with what she thinks or what I think? What if we don't want the same thing or we do, but we think there are different ways to get it?

What does feminism do in this moment?

In the meantime, how should I feel about him?

When I do it, when it's me at the bar—leaning in—how is it different?

Is it different?

And when it's me at the bar, with a strange hand resting on the small of my back—how is it different?

Is it different?

I've read articles about men and what we should do with them/about them/without them, where they belong, and what they deserve. I've taken classes and considered so many crowded intersections that it eventually led me to a crossroads.

I've been touched without an ask and I've been chased down a street by a man whose advances I refused. I've had my life threatened at home and on public transit. I've been the victim of circumstances I was warned about by matriarchs and media my entire life. I've been wrong about men and wronged by them, too.

Also, I've been believed in by men, helped by men, heard by men, seen by men, held accountable by men, loved by men.

There are men who are some of my favorite people in this world, the kind of human beings I'm so glad to have found on this planet, to know in this life. Not despite what they are, but because of who they are.

There have been moments recently when I've told other friends or people I've dated or strangers that, often, I find that my most intimate friendships have been with men, and they've looked at me like I am fighting against myself. Like I need to work through something—a trauma, or an unclaimed identity, or the absence of my father.

But because women casually share articles on how to stay safe while in a parking lot or at a party or while walking down the street or riding in an Uber or in a public bathroom or at school or while sleeping in your home or whenever you're around strangers or partners or family, and a number to call when he loses his job or when he drinks too much or when his team loses the big game, I know where the look is coming from, why the intimacy is a surprise.

Because I am a friend of men, I have also had to ask myself some questions. Questions about what I'm like now and what I would be like with different options, a bigger allowance.

I have to ask myself: What if I could build a world that protects me from my own insecurities? Makes everything I think and do the most important thing to think and do? What if I could believe myself more worthy of life and choice and time and understanding than anyone else?

Would I be him instead of me?

Is this why I've forgiven him instead of holding him accountable?

Am I me because I can't be him? Or am I me because I don't want to be? Because I never want to be doing the most I can get away with?

I have to ask myself the questions: Haven't I figured out a million ways to be forgiven? Haven't I tried to build a world that protects me from my own insecurities? Haven't I tried to make everything I think and do the most important thing to think and do? Haven't I believed myself more worthy of life and choice and time and understanding than other people? Not out of my identities, but out of my own fear. As a way to feel more powerful.

Sometimes we protect parasitic men by pretending there is a benefit, mutualism.

Sometimes we protect men who are obvious emergencies. The ones we allow ourselves to feel responsible for, take on as a way of knowing something about ourselves.

Sometimes we protect them out of closeness. Because we like or love them. Because we knew or know them.

Because the one we love—the one we thought we knew best—is the entitled one, who stopped doing what he *should* do to do what he's allowed to do instead.

Sometimes we protect ourselves from the inconvenience of hard decisions, conversations.

*

WE'LL BELIEVE IT when it's true.

Maybe not even then.

Dear black people,

Why do we care? What are we trying to prove to them? Why are we engaging in a 24/7 dialogue with white people and calling it self-love? Perhaps white people still know more about what we're capable of than we do.

Because here we are in a constant state of "Look, see, look! We can run, we can read, we can swim, we can think, we can go and do and see and be! Hey, white people! We told you, didn't we? Look! Please look at us so that it counts, because it doesn't count unless you're seeing it. We must prove everything to you because you are the standard. The call to our response. And we're a desperate, grinning version of whatever it is that you think you are."

And it's kind of weird, isn't it? They used to keep us in their game with threats and violence. Literally enslave us in it. Now we run back to it and call it success. Achievement. It's an accomplishment if they want us. We've worked side by side with white people to reshape our black reality into something sharp around the edges. This way, we can remain scared of stepping over what is immediately visible and into a version of ourselves that is more than race, rhetoric, rage, and reaction. Even better, when one of us is brave enough to endure the sharpness and attempt the unknown, we can call it a cultural betrayal and drag them. Back.

And yet.

We used to escape deep into the woods—the twisted darkness of southern expanse late at night—hoping not to get caught. Now we're even deeper in the woods in the middle of the day, praying that they discover us. That they notice. Waiting for an invitation to our own self-hatred, asking, "What took you so long? Why didn't you notice me sooner?"

—*Jillisblack*, September 20, 2017

FLOWERS FOR THE BLACK ARTISTS

in which the liberals, through their foundation, choose eight artists to retreat for a week on the coast in two four-bedroom houses.

in which the (nice, rich, white) liberals, through their (nice, white, liberal arts) foundation, choose eight (black) artists to retreat for a week on the coast in two four-bedroom houses.

in which the (nice, rich, white) liberals (colonizers with a heart of gold), through their (nice, white, liberal arts) foundation (tax shelter) choose (gift as a charitable deduction) eight (black) artists to (receive money / time / opportunity / access) retreat (passively network) for a week on the coast in two four-bedroom houses (off-season Airbnbs).

Of the eight (black) artists, two are writers.

I am the one who writes essays (about being black).

The other writes screenplays about (black) kids who are (also) robots.

The screenwriter, the painter, the muralist, the illustrator, the actress, the performance artist, the mixed-media artist, and the essayist.

The black artists are here doing the black arts, remember?
Oh, that's right, that's right.
They're artists.
That's good, that's good. Okay, good. Good for them.

When I arrive, I am assigned a room in the blue house—the one closer to the shops but farther from the ocean. In my room, there is minimal furniture. A twin bed with a nautical throw pillow, a blue-striped wingback armchair, a wooden bookshelf filled with white classics and a dutiful show copy of *Beloved*, the pages still crisp and tidy, unturned. In front of a large bay window, there is a writing desk, and on that desk there are blue and purple begonias arranged in a glass vase. Tucked underneath the vase is a small white envelope, a card inside that reads:

Jill,
Before the masterpiece, we must master peace! We hope you enjoy your time here, and that it inspires within you a willingness to be great!

I rest the card on the desk, sit on the bed, call my mother to let her know that I've arrived, wonder if all the artists got the same flowers or if mine were individually chosen. Like I was.

*

THAT NIGHT, WE are all welcomed to the coast by a man from the arts foundation. He smiles when he talks, apologizes for things that don't matter. We offer back to him things he gave us in the first place—a seat, a plate of the catered food, a bottle of water. He says he just wants to get out of there and leave us to it, whatever it is, but he'll see us on Saturday for the community Q&A.

"The people who live here are so happy to have you, and they're very excited to hear all about your art," he says.

Jill, we can't wait to hear all about how our racism influences your art.

If you make us feel guilty enough, we'll call you brave for your efforts.

You can't make us love blackness, but you can make us love the way you use it.

How will you use it?

On the walls are childhood photos of the homeowner's now-adult children. They spent their summers here, their growth spurts recorded on the door frame in permanent marker, meant to stay.

After he leaves, we convene in the yellow house for dinner. We sit around the dining room table with the curtains wide open on a window that belongs to them but is temporarily full of us instead: the screenwriter, the painter, the muralist, the illustrator, the actress, the performance artist, the mixed-media artist, and the essayist.

We squeeze in close, make just enough room for everyone to have a seat. We eat our catered food off their cobalt blue ceramic dishes, drink donated red wine out of their cups.

As it grows dark outside, the ocean view becomes implied, and we become less implied. We are reflected back to ourselves in the glass under the dim light of a low-hanging fixture, more easily seen by the neighbors walking their dogs or walking themselves around the neighborhood. We leave rings of donated red wine on their real-wood tabletop, talk and laugh so loudly that the porcelain teacups and family heirlooms rattle nervously in the cabinet, unused to so much vitality and bass.

We sit on display, swirl the wine, talk about what it means to be black artists (preservation).

They use us, steal our work, force us to compromise.

But how else can we get our art out into the world?

How else can our story be heard?

I mean, we have to do it, right?

Yeah, we have to do it.
It just sucks that we have to do it like this.
It does. It really does.
But it's worth it.
Oh, it's totally worth it.
All we have to do is take the cheese without disturbing the trap.
Easy.

We talk about what it's like to be nice white liberals (speculation). To live in this town without having a real big special talent, influence, or fame. To live here not as a somebody but as an anybody.

Oh, but what's it like?
To be you.
To be black.
Like you.
Write us a book.
Sing us a song.
Make us a movie.
About you.
That's really about us.
And the thrill.
And the bravery.
Of your soulful
Persistence.
We're paying you.

Sitting around that table, we don't talk about *the feeling*.

Instead, we go around the table and talk about the art that brought us to the coast. It seems like, in every case, blackness brought us to the art. I'm so curious about each of us. I'm so curious about us.

We are the chosen black artists.

We are "recently awarded," "semi-influential," "well educated," "sponsored by," "in conversation with," "newly important fresh takes and reverse spins." Here "on behalf of" everyone else. Everyone else who may or may no longer concern us.

We are the chosen black artists, taking up temporary residency in places where white people can afford to slow down, breathe, stay for good.

I listen to the painter, the illustrator, the actress, the performance artist. And when I speak, I sound like everyone else.

I talk in long monologues, answer questions about myself that no one asked. I like for my name to be known, and I like to mention other people's names, too.

I like to tell an intimate story about my personal relationship with a public figure. I like to be given credit for showing/knowing/being/spinning something shiny and bright. I like to be stunning and prolific and devastating. I like to let everyone know that I'm here.

I am the overbearing parent of brainchildren and pet projects. I wax poetic about the black body. I will accept my reparations in the form of recognition. I crave the spotlight and I hope remaining seen can save me. I'll express myself into the great beyond.

If I lived in this town, I would have no special occasion or collective camouflage to save me. There would be no other black person to pay the price for my compromise. No black person who could've easily been me instead. I would be immediately identifiable, the only one mistaking myself for someone else.

And even though I'm not, I tell them that I'm working on a book. What's true is that I'm working my way up to a book, trying to stop pretending that I don't want the things I want. That's why I'm here.

As the next bottle of wine is passed and the mixed-media artist starts talking about making heads from headlines—I wonder what the point of a book would be.

If we could move enough units of something to live here, become a big-enough somebody to feel safe enough, we'd have to live in isolation, away from everything that is ours, the only one or two of something, their reminder of what's out there, what they're rich enough to get away from—with the exception of this one week, this one time.

This is their home.

We are the black artists.

Doing our black arts.

Resting our weary heads and tired minds for a week in someone else's summer hideaway, the black people with the permission slip.

There's an art to getting one, but that's not the art we say we're here to do, because that's the art that makes us feel the guiltiest.

And we're not here to feel guilty.

We're here to do the art.

We don't do it for the money. We don't need the applause. We don't need anyone to notice what we've made. We just want it, that's all. We deserve it, that's all. If we were white, we'd have it already. That's all.

I want it because if I were them, I'd have it.

*

THE NEXT MORNING, I sit in the backyard around the wrought-iron table with the chipping white paint and drink my coffee with the performance artist and the screenwriter. I ask them what kind of flowers were waiting in their rooms when they arrived.

The performance artist shrugs. "I don't remember."

The screenwriter shrugs. "Roses, I think."

They talk industry politics, gatekeepers, people they know who they think can get them in front of the right person.

I drink my coffee and watch them, always happy to observe and archive, until the screenwriter turns to me and smiles, says, "Jill, what are you working on here?"

"Essays."

"Yeah? Cool, cool. Smart."

"Yeah, thank you. You're working on the screenplay about kid robots, right?"

"Well, no. That one is being shopped right now. The one that I'm working on here is about these two friends—one is black and the other one is white. The black friend ends up at an Ivy League, becomes this super successful lawyer, and the white one drops out of high school and ends up on drugs."

"Oh, I see."

"Yeah, and then eventually the white guy ends up on trial for shooting a cop and the black guy takes his case."

"Dope," the performance artist says.

"The ol' switcheroo," I say, sipping my coffee.

The screenwriter looks at me, confused. "What do you mean?"

I excuse myself.

*

LATER THAT AFTERNOON, I take a long walk around town, note the architecture and the tension.

If I wanted this—the big house with the American flag and the tree swing in the small coastal town, I would be jealous of the seasoned air, the sound of continuous disturbance across the water, the nonsymmetrical facades and the steep gabled roofs, the little post office and the novelty shops, the white wine glasses clinking and the loud laughter. I would feel slighted.

If this were it—if the laughter didn't require the wine and the waves on the water weren't a reminder of friction—I would bury myself under all the lives that will never be mine and contaminate the soil with the acid of my blame/envy.

Or maybe I would want to run back to that house that isn't mine either and figure out a way to make the nice white liberals listen to me, buy my book, read my words.

Maybe I would want to sit down at their desk, the sun streaming in through the window and illuminating the dust (dirt, bacteria, pollutants, hair, decomposing insects, dead skin), and figure out a new way to say the same thing about the latest version of an ongoing problem, *speak on behalf of.*

Maybe I would insert myself in their collection, twist and turn the tired themes like keys in the door of a house near the sea where the bones have settled south and been forgotten about and the stench is hidden underneath the pretense, dead fish, and salt water and no one has to admit to anything—with the exception of a small plaque on a side street that sums it all up in a regrettable but ultimately necessary history. I would want to do that, too. I would summarize my regrets with the same words that satisfy my needs.

I would.

But also, I will.

Because I'm here, too.

The old switcheroo.

*

THAT NIGHT, I go out to dinner with the screenwriter, the painter, and the muralist. The owner smiles, waves us in excitedly as we are seated by the host.

The restaurant is located in the renovated home of a sea captain and is a shared-plate dining, cocktails with rose syrup, modern rustic, updated Mediterranean gastropub with sea-and-sand globe glass pendants hanging over each small table from the factory-weathered plank-wood ceilings kind of place.

Twenty pairs of watchful eyes pan, zoom in on us like dome security cameras, capture us from every angle.

They seat us directly in the middle of the restaurant, and while the screenwriter, the painter, and the muralist consider appetizers, I can't help but surveil the surveillants. Notice them notice us out of both curiosity and concern, having vigilance in common.

We sit around that table center stage, faces bobbing in and out of view, in or out of the shadows being created by a precariously dancing flame, and declare ourselves the winners. We don't care if they don't want us here. We don't care because, *goddamnit*, we're here!

We're here.

Chosen.

Yeah, fuck that.

We don't have to be wanted.

We just have to be here.

Preserving our bodies through our bodies of work.

Feared or, worse, trusted.

We don't care.

Fuck them.

And when dinner is over, we walk back to the house and talk more shit, and eventually we go to their rooms and quickly fall asleep in their beds. I feel like a kid coming down from a tantrum.

*

ON THE FOURTH day, I learn that the actress had daffodils in her room—which she happens not to like. I also learn that she is writing a play about her life.

"Will you be playing yourself?" I ask, as we sit outside in the matching white Adirondack chairs, sipping our coffee in unison.

"Definitely," she says.

She tells me about the industry, how she's had to fight for every single part she's gotten, how all the interesting roles go to the white actresses, how she can only ever play a friend or a coworker, a maid or an enslaved woman.

"Or like, somebody's baby mama or the ratchet black chick. You know, the stereotypes. And I graduated from Tisch, okay? Tell me why the fuck I got formally trained to play a stereotype?"

The man who lives in the house across the street opens the front door for his dog, who quickly finds his scent, reclaims his territory, runs back inside behind his owner.

"What's your ideal role?" I ask.

"This one. The one that I'm writing now. The play itself is all about my experiences in predominantly white spaces. Because I was one of *those* black girls, you know. I grew up in an all-white neighborhood, I went to prep school. I was on the rowing team, for fuck's sake! You know what I'm saying? And when I'd meet other black girls out in the world, I would be all excited like, 'Yay! Finally, someone who will understand me!' But they didn't like me because they thought I was stuck-up, or maybe they thought I thought I was better than them or something because of how I talked or because I was doing stuff that white girls did. But I was just being myself."

She shrugs, smirks.

"Did you?" I ask.

"Did I what?"

"Did you think that you were better than them?"

"No, I just thought I was different than them."

"Because you're a role that requires formal training."

She nods at me, smiles.

"You get it," she says.

I find a way to excuse myself.

*

OF THE EIGHT black artists, I am the only one who started on social media.

It's like I've done something backward. Cheated somehow. Because I wasn't chosen by an industry.

I was chosen by an algorithm.

And everything important that happens now, happens after that.

The other artists resent social media, say it ruins everything.

People don't have to be good anymore, you know?

People don't have to make real art.

People can get ten thousand likes off of nothing.

Artists have to actually be good to get noticed.

Artists have to put in the work.

Artists have to perfect their craft.

Now they want to ask us how many followers we have?

Are you fucking serious?

But not you, Jill.

Your account is different.

I tell them that it's not and they laugh.

Of course it is. Or else you wouldn't be here.

*

ON THE FIFTH night, I sit on the back porch with the muralist and smoke a joint.

"What kind of flowers were in your room when you got here?" I ask him.

"White lilies from the lily-whites," he says, laughing and coughing, "if you can fucking believe it."

He passes it to me and I watch the smoke rise in the darkness, suspend, disappear. I inhale into an escape and exhale into an answer. "I can absolutely fucking believe it."

We laugh, and I pass it back to him.

"What's it like for you in this town?" I ask him.

He sits up, scratches at his beard, "It's a little bit weird, but it's cool out here, you know? It's peaceful."

"What's it like walking around as a tall black man?"

He shrugs. "I mean, I'm definitely getting some stares out here, right? But like, of course. That's everywhere. For the most part, though, everybody I've encountered around town has been really cool. Friendly."

"Do you think it's because they know what we're here for?"

"Maybe. I don't care why they're being friendly, to be honest. I just want them to keep doing it. I don't want any problems. Shit, I speak to them first! They're probably like, 'Damn, who is that friendly black guy waving at us from across the street?' But they wave back!" he says, laughing.

I laugh, too. But I start to feel paranoid as we rock in the owner's chairs, haloed by the porch light and obscured by the smoke we make.

"I've never heard quiet like this in my whole life," he says. "Where I live, it's always loud."

"Will you ever leave New York?" I ask, already certain of his answer.

He shakes his head. "Probably not. I like the energy of it, the pace, the culture. The food. *Us.* That's home, you know? I don't think I could ever really leave and be happy. I'd miss all the things that made me who I am. That remind me of who I am."

We sit in silence for a moment, passing the joint back and forth until it burns into an end.

I excuse myself.

*

ON THE DAY of the (Black) Artist Community Q&A, the two writers, the mixed-media artist, the performance artist, the screenwriter, the actress, the muralist, and the illustrator get all dressed up to go on display. It's time to show and tell what the permission slip, the quiet, and the ocean got us/them. What we came away with and what it's worth. How we earned our temporary keep.

The event is hosted by a (white) painter who lives in a contemporary Georgian-style house right on the edge of a retro downtown and a seemingly limitless sea. All the furniture in the living room has been moved to one side to accommodate resident artists and aesthete residents.

As promised, the man from the arts foundation is back for the pudding. This time, he's joined by several colleagues who walk around the spacious living room making small talk with each artist, asking questions about schools and travel, presumed poverty and amusing privileges.

I find myself watching the waves crash through a sashed window with no curtains and no blinds, waiting to be saved by the pure force of my own awkwardness, as a man from the foundation engages me in a conversation about trying to force the artistic process, whether or not it is truly possible.

He has a friendly mustache and wears a silly tie instead of a serious one to let us know that he's different from the rest of them. Maybe he participated in a sit-in once or had his own run-ins once or twice, but either way, he's only working this job to help people like me. To keep the rooms fair for when we can't be there. He has the kind of smile that I once believed but disbelieve now. Mostly because I disbelieve myself whenever I'm around one.

Away from. On behalf of.

Pretending not to know what I'm doing.

Jill, you can justify absolutely anything for the promise of enough money or enough recognition.

Enough time to be alone and gather your thoughts.

They're going to use you anyway. Jill, why not go for the thing that you always wanted—that thing that's so expensive? Health insurance, maybe. They're going to use you anyway.

Jill, your mother deserves everything because she did it without anyone else. Your brother deserves everything because they tried to sit him in a hallway in an Alabama elementary school and forget about him. Let them use you because you could really use the money. Let them smile at you and feed you and fill your room with begonias. Let them give you a break. Let them feel good for seeing something in you. Yes, you already know how it'll go. But maybe you can figure out how to do both well.

Jill, it's not like you want much. How much does it take? You just want to be okay, right? You want to go to the dentist once a year, not worry so much about not having enough. Maybe you can be the one person who makes it out of a lie alive.

Artists have to eat.

Right?

I come with new and old injuries, recently burned fingertips and aging stab wounds that I like to forget about whenever I want something. Whenever I want to ascend to a new level of complicity but call it curiosity instead.

They flare up sometimes.

Jill, are you going to write a book about being complicit just so that you can feel better about being complicit?

But Silly Tie doesn't ask me that question.

He asks, "The only way to do it is a writing schedule, don't you think? A few pages every morning."

Maybe he doesn't ask because he already knows that my presence is my answer.

"Sure, I agree," I say.

I think Silly Tie wants me to articulate my thoughts on being a . . .

Black. *Queer.* <u>Woman</u>. Born in Oakland!!! Raised in ALABAMA. The child of a *single parent.* The sister of a **black man**. Living in a <u>*low-income*</u> apartment when she goes #VIRAL!!! (The later generation of a black family who worships money and materialism. Degrees. Whose coldness will often remind her of why what she wants won't work. Can't preserve.)

Work on wanting less.

To pay off the debt, I will write of the time I spent by the sea, the long walks in the afternoon among the welcoming locals and tiny nautical gift shops, gathering the output of all my big thoughts and important musings, tapping the tree of suffering for sap. Then I will be worth my weight in flowers.

"Do you write in the morning?" he asks, smiling underneath the very hairy situation.

"Not yet, no. But I'd like to start."

"Well, when have you been writing here?"

Sometimes (most times) I need the pressure of waiting till it's almost too late to force me into a sentence of accidental honesty. But that's not what he wants to hear.

"I'm one of those people who writes all night. I like to do it in the dark," I say, rocking on my heels and sipping white wine.

The truth is, I'm in bed every night by 9:30, exhausted from small talk and sun rays, the ins and outs of pretending not to sweat.

Before he can respond, we're interrupted by an announcement that the Q&A session is about to begin, and the (chosen black) artists are asked if they could kindly approach the front of the room and take their assigned seats.

I politely nod an "excuse me" at Silly Tie and make my way over to where the dark row splits the room. I find my name at the very end of the line, the chair closest to the door.

We are asked a series of questions about what our art requires of us and what we require of ourselves. We are asked about recurring themes.

Do current events show up in our work?

Childhoods?

We don't want to be the thing that you are.

We just want to know what it's like.

Take this money.

You can be our entertainment.

You've always been so good.

At making us cry.

At making us laugh.

At fascinating us.
You make us feel.
Like we can do anything.
Tell us what we are.
Tell us what we're like from the outside.
Tell us what we're like from your insides.
Give us that good gospel.
That old-time religion.
That soul food.
Or subvert it.
Freak it.
Remember everything you do
That surprises us
Is actually just the us
In you.
Clever, different.
Ironic.
Look, you're living in the big house.
For a week.
Make your reality.
Art.
(Is that preservation
Too?)

Arts programs come up. Arts programs in schools with diverse student bodies. Diverse student bodies. The importance of a break. The importance of a foundation.

Then we are asked to show or talk about what we've worked on since arriving.

When it is my turn, I smile at the audience, make a joke about the small problem of having *too* much time on my hands and *too* much beauty at my fingertips to write at length about the woes of the world.

They laugh.

I tell them that I'm only kidding, that I've begun working on what will be the beginning of my first book. I open the Google Doc that last saved just three hours ago, and read to them from an essay about Langston Hughes's house and of a choice finally being made in real time.

Dear Jillisblack,

Where are you? Like, hasn't anyone ever told you how social media works? Hasn't anyone told you that trauma is trending and you can sell consciousness for capital these days? Like, do it!

And you're commercial, which is code for classism, so don't you want to further develop your brand? The awkward aesthetic, the self-righteousness? Colorism helps, of course. And the white liberals think you're a challenge, so you can work that angle, too. That's great!

But Jill, you have to post. You've got to know and then grow and then unknow and outgrow your audience into more online relevance and popularity. Jill, there's sooo much race stuff you could be reacting to right now, like, so many quality racial topics. So, like, react. Reactions are shareable, and that's good for your account. And your videos were better when they started with "Dear white people," because it made your market more obvious. And this hipster accountability thing is cute, but where's it going? Like, where is your book? Where is your podcast? Don't you want to be verified? Don't you want to sell contrived

authenticity like a product? Where's your pack-
aging and solutions for your version of media
visibility?

This is real life, you know?

So where are you?

—*Jillisblack*, April 9, 2018

LET THE LITTLE PEOPLE THROUGH

It's just barely summer in the South Carolina suburbs, and even though your mother's mammoth sunflowers are starting to grow uncomfortably tall in the small backyard and the same three songs are drifting from the wide-open window of a standard-size SUV by noon and the air is reeking of sweat, smoke, and watermelon-scented chemicals by the time the sun sets behind haunted trees and chain restaurants, it's just barely a summer.

Everything that's selling out fast is antiviral or antiracist or—with a talented PR team—both, and people are wearing their masks in public, just in case they are found out to be a loud or silent carrier of one of the things that no one wants.

Breathing around each other has become dangerous, so I CAN'T BREATHE masks are all sold out online, and the popular race-forward books with the stern covers and marketable titles are on the shelves or in the tote bags of the guilty left in need of a cause or a conundrum and the trendy middle in need of a script or a scapegoat and the retired Unitarians in need of a title or a toolkit.

We're stuck inside with ourselves, trying to believe the things we're supposed to think and to mean the things we're supposed to say. We're performing interpersonal politics in public, more conscientious than conscious, systematic in our approach, same or shame, safe or sorry. What's the difference?

We've caught ourselves in the traps we set for other people's contradictions, and finding no logical way out, we almost always give in.

Your marriage has ended and you've left Atlanta. Traveled up north to a different type of South. You're living with your mother in a house that's like all the other houses around it for miles. There are rosebushes in front, a friendly doormat, a spring-themed flag.

Your stepfather lives there, too.

You're living in the kind of compromise that capitalism creates. The kind that feels like the latter years of your childhood, after your single mother of one got married and became a single mother of two, but with a husband.

You lived in a different neighborhood then, on a winding drive of character houses and holiday decorations, block parties and trampolines, in another small southern town where college football is an ethic, and anything different is deviant, divisive, dangerous. You were the new black family on an established white street—a husband, a wife, a brother, a sister. Allowable only because you appear safe, aligned, malleable.

*

AT THE BUS stop, the other sixth graders ask if that guy is your real dad. They ask you where your real dad is then. They ask if you like boys, because you don't really seem like you do. Which boy do you like then?

When your stepfather feels entitled to the spoils of his rage, and you must drive the half hour to your grandmother's house to spend the night, your grandmother calls your stepfather a good choice. Former military and a college graduate—the kind of college graduate that references it often, thinks of it as a kind of earned worthiness, a bulletproof vest—he is perceived as a safe and, thus, good, choice. Because he played football, joined a black fraternity, got a job, kept a job, he was a good choice.

Respectability makes him a good choice.

Your grandmother says forgive him and stay, and the next time she says forgive him and stay, and the next time she says, "You all have a beautiful house. I really think it's best you stay."

You already have an idea, but this confirms that money is important, and you start to wish you had more money than your stepfather so that you could win instead. So that people would give you the benefit of the doubt instead. So that he could move again instead. So that he could start over with nothing again instead.

*

BUT NOW, YEARS later, it's different. Now your step-father quotes CNN, tucks his short-sleeved company polo shirt into wide-legged khakis, watches reruns of *Becker*. He still works in middle management, calls the people who work for him thugs and idiots. Most of his stories are about work or alcohol.

As long as you've known him, he's needed to live in hell to feel at home. He's performed masculinity as abuse. He's yelled whenever someone was unwilling to lie for him, see him as he needs to see himself. He's yelled whenever he thinks someone has forgotten that he *can*, that he still knows how.

For half a year, he stays mostly quiet.

But you know it's coming.

It's the early half of an already hot Sunday when he stands in the living room and recites with a smirk, "You know, these cops are out here killing up black men in the street like it's nothing. It's dangerous out here for us. A real shame, honestly." He keeps smirking and staring and waiting for a response, and you realize that the words aren't said as information but rather as some sort of explanation for who and what he is.

But you already know. He's shown you.

So there is nothing to say. All your personal thoughts about him are in conflict with all your political thoughts about men like him whom you'll never actually know, whose secrets you haven't been keeping, and men you love, whom you've chosen, who are unlearning their way out of normalized abuse, too.

A week later the man from next door, with the three young boys and the wife who loves being a substitute teacher, is working on one of his antique cars in his standard white subdivision garage, a tiny radio playing only your favorite country hits from yesterday and today, and he's wiping the sweat from his brow with a stack of Dunkin' Donuts napkins. The man from the other next door, with the oxygen tank and the hot tub, is chain-smoking cigarettes on his covered patio. You're standing in the living room. *Poetic Justice* is on BET again—all the profanity has been removed to protect the innocence of neglected children—and your stepfather is on the other end of the phone. He and the alcohol are calmly informing you that they're on their way home to kill you and your mother.

Suddenly you are wide awake again. Back from that lie you tell yourself when you need to pretend that what you forgive, you deserve again.

And at the very same time, all around you, there's George Floyd as headline. George Floyd as topic. George Floyd as symbol. George Floyd as Sunday sermon. George Floyd as political tactic. George Floyd as distant idea. George Floyd as COLE SPROUSE AND KAIA GERBER REUNITE FOR BLACK LIVES MATTER MARCH AFTER HE DENIES THEY'RE DATING. George Floyd as KATHERINE HEIGL ON DISCUSSING GEORGE FLOYD'S DEATH WITH HER DAUGHTER: "HOW WILL I EXPLAIN THE UNEXPLAINABLE?" George Floyd as martyr. George Floyd as catalyst for change. George Floyd as *too hard too sad too far too obvious too public*. George Floyd as behind our reusable masks we are all the same. George Floyd as sacrifice. George Floyd as necessary. George Floyd as matter, moment, history.

Matter: Anything that occupies space.

Your stepfather is black and your stepfather is a man. He is himself, too. Your stepfather harms and your step-father's been harmed. He is a product and a consumer. In exchange for clean breaks, and out of our own discom-fort with our own humanness, we desire a perfect victim, a silent hero. We play God to find godliness. We ignore the details, uncomfortable with two or more things being true at the same time—not *right*, but *true*.

Real.

And in that moment, in the living room, where you are standing with your mother, as Chicago slaps Iesha in front of a beautiful overlook and whatever she says in response has been replaced with a more appropriate word, your childhood seeks a conclusion to a lingering story.

You and your mother fill the car with as many important things as it can hold, throw some clothes and toiletries into overnight bags, and when you're done, you leave in the dark with your dog to go stay in a room at the Country Inn and Suites where the shower doesn't work and the pool is right outside your window, bright blue surrounded by yellow caution tape, closed until further notice.

As the pool lights glow behind a curtain that won't close all the way, you both decide that it's time to go back to Washington. You miss the weed and the weather, the mountains and the trees. You miss the health care and the coffee. You miss the kind of racism that smiles at you first, plays you a few chords of something by Bikini Kill on an acoustic guitar that it doesn't even bother tuning, lies after.

You leave the news on just for the noise and wake up to different versions of the same story. *Another corporation has taken to Twitter to agree that #BlackLivesMatter. Businesses are starting to reopen, but is it too much too soon? In response to the protests, there are curfews in place across the country. Did you hear what Trump said? Did you see what he did?*

That first day, you head immediately west, away from the Spanish moss that hangs limply from the trees and the plantations that are now tourist attractions. You've told almost no one that you are driving cross-country. You don't want to hear the requisite fear in their voices, sense the concern in their texts. You don't need to be reminded of the virus, the protests, the mandates, the masks. You can't stay home because home isn't safe. The immediate trouble is inside, just as terrifying as anything else that wants you dead.

The last two days in the hotel, there had hardly been any time to think about anything else other than getting to Washington. You ship three boxes to your brother in Marblemount, organize the car, plan your route on Google Maps, review your combined budget, buy a few travel-friendly groceries, fold a few feelings neatly away until there is more time to try them on, decide what still fits.

And yet, there is George Floyd standing six feet away from you in the grocery store as you are smiled at by a man in uniform. George Floyd is in the tension outside, the humidity. He is in the reminder you give yourself in a hotel bathtub after you try to cry about one of the many things that's happened in the past forty-eight hours and can't. You remind yourself to look around, take it all in, move it around until you make it make as much sense as it ever can.

Because there is no way to avoid being black in America. There is no right time to travel. There is nowhere safer to be instead. And there is no time to waste. There is no old or new normal. If it's all fucked, then let it find you.

Whatever catches you, let it catch you in motion.

You drive your way through a few of Tennessee's forgotten exits, past the old Ford trucks with the fading support ribbons on the bumper, the gas stations with the peeling red racer stripes, the little black firecracker stands covered in dripping neon announcements, the flags and the crosses, the crumbling identities of forgotten whiteness, always holding on to itself so tightly that it breaks. Privilege taps you on your shoulder and asks where the fuck you are.

You steer the silver Hyundai Elantra that now holds almost everything you and your mother own in the world over the mountains and out of the sweaty grip of an angry white America that thinks it still has a chance against data, diversity, and digital. Still sees itself as more of a race than a concept, system, trap. An angry white America that hopeful white America finds loud, embarrassing, that it fights with at holiday dinners after one too many glasses of wine, that it unfollows on social media. An angry white America that hopeful white America blames for everything it doesn't like about itself.

That first night, you're in between large towns and too far away from the cities when it almost gets too dark. You stop at an exit that's almost the kind of exit you were looking for and check into a Quality Inn that sits right next door to a truck stop and across the street from a Huddle House.

The woman at the front desk behind the makeshift Plexiglas wall and superstore-size hand sanitizer sees your driver's license and asks if you're from Washington.

"California originally," you say, and even though it's true, it sounds like you're lying.

"Me too. I'm from California," she says, and your eyebrows lift without permission.

Now you both sound like you're lying.

"Oh yeah? What part?"

"Southern California. Like, right outside of San Diego."

"Ah, I'm from up north," you tell her. But she's never been, says it was never a place she needed to see.

She hands you your room keys through a hole in the Plexiglas and shows you where the ice machines are on the hotel map, circles them with a black Sharpie, just in case.

"You're all set," she says, smiling. "And in case I don't see you again, have a good rest of your trip."

It takes you too long to reorganize your wallet, too long to fold the receipt, find the card keys in your pocket, so you ask her how she ended up in Clarksville.

"I couldn't take California anymore. I miss it. I have family there still and I miss my family. But I love it here. It's easy and it's quiet. There aren't a whole lot of choices to make and nobody bothers you. In San Diego there was always something to go do. I always had somewhere I had to be. I moved here and there's not much to do and

I don't have too many places to be. Nobody is paying attention to us out here. Nobody cares what we're doing."

The next morning you walk your dog in the small plot of grass with the restless flies and the discarded Styrofoam. You are carefully observed by a trucker who doesn't smile back and someone who is sitting on the sidewalk, lazily smoking a cigarette and swatting the bugs away with a plastic hotel cup. And because you've lived as you for a long time now, you know that the staring can be about all or some of the many things that you are and how those things work with all or some of the many things they are.

When you get back to the room, you tell your mother about the staring. The vibe in the parking lot is off, and it's probably fine but, well, you know. It is, until.

Joe Biden is on the television talking about how "he was the guy in the room who always said . . ."

And the black political correspondents are on the cable news stations telling white political correspondents that they don't know what it's like to be black in this country.

But how can they ever know what it's like to know what it's like?

It doesn't matter.

Matter: Be of importance; have significance.

It's more lucrative to educate hopeful white people forever, to tell them that they can never know but you can teach them how to be better learners for $19.99/month. And it's more lucrative to come up with the curriculum, sell it to the hopeful whites so they can eventually sell it to everyone else. Make them an expert in what they can never know. Let them decide which of you is more of an expert in articulating an experience they can never have. Let them share you on Instagram with the caption: "Fellow white people, watch this. It's important."

But how do they know what's important about it if they can't even know who's telling the truth? If black people don't all agree, then how do white people decide which black people to listen to? What do they base it on—their agreement?

Your mother drives you out of Tennessee and farther into the middle of the country, where you are surrounded by nothing but America. On the outskirts of the outskirts, you mostly encounter windmills and crosses. Little square houses dot the side of the highway, and you try to imagine what it's like to live in the blue one with the broken swing set and the KEEP AMERICA GREAT sign in the front yard. What it's like to live within the whiteness that whiteness doesn't want, in a house with a yard sign that reads as one thing but means "Fuck you," in a town that's aging with you, where things close more than they open, where there is no one left to meet and nothing left to do.

But you can't. And you don't really want to.

A child stands in the front yard of the blue house with the swing set and the sign, holding hands with a white-haired adult and waving at the cars. You wave because when you've started denying yourself the enjoyment of your own humanity, then you've lost something vital. Something that doesn't feel theoretical. The child and the adult wave back excitedly, smile from being noticed, and it makes you happy even if it's not supposed to—not right now while your truth is defined by your dedication to anger. And maybe it's because they aren't wearing masks that you notice their smiles anyway.

Because you're supposed to know that when you wave, they win. *Fuck that,* the voices that are meant to keep you safe/sane say. *They don't give a fuck about us. What the fuck do you look like waving at one of their kids? They don't give a fuck about our kids, Jill! You must hate yourself to do some smiling-ass, Uncle Tom–ass, coon-ass shit like that. Do you hate yourself? Do you know your history? You think these white people really give a fuck about you? Did that white cop give a fuck about George Floyd? That white kid's going to grow up right there in that town and become the kind of white adult that shoots you in broad daylight like it's nothing, and you have the audacity to wave, you fucking traitor. What you forgive, you deserve. Don't you remember?*

You're supposed to know, or else you don't get it. But also, there are some exceptions.

You can wave if the waving makes you the president. You can wave if the waving makes you a global superstar with a global superstar husband. You can wave if your other hand is full of money, if your compromise has made you a resource.

But don't wave at that child who can't pay you or put you on.

Save your hands for the exceptions, for the opportunities too big to miss.

In front of you there is nothing but flatland split in the middle by straight road. Behind you are the white people who live in a house on the highway, with a view of everything they can already see. They're still waving in the wind like a flag.

If no one wants it, do we still call it privilege?

You stop for the night outside Kansas City, Kansas, or Kansas City, Missouri. You never figure out which one. In the morning, you walk your dog around a park that's right outside the hotel. There's a walking trail, a lake in the middle, geese in the lake, a roundabout. Middle-class details. Your dog is pulling on the leash, but she's cute, harmless, so the other people with dogs smile when she lunges at them. You shrug dramatically, laugh, play the part of "Who owns who here?!"

"She always tries to embarrass me in public. I don't know why she's like this," you say cheerfully, playing hopeless. And they smile at you with an empathy reserved for certain roles you know to play.

They say, "Don't worry. We have small dogs at home. What's her name?"

They never ask you yours and you never ask them theirs, and when you stop making small talk and say goodbye, you all wave at the dogs. Say their names, instead.

Then everyone smiles, masks around their necks.

That day, you'll make it to Colorado and that's all you care about. It *sounds* like something different from the South, from Middle America—even if it's not. You expect the scenery to change as you grow closer, but there is still just wind blowing red dust and flat earth meeting wide sky up until you finally cross the line and Google Maps says, "Welcome." The hotel sits between a cornfield and a gas station, and when you open the window in your room, the smell of manure wafts in and stays.

You eat sandwiches and drink red wine out of plastic hotel cups, and neither of you can figure out a way to say "Can you believe that we're here? Can you believe what had to happen?" with enough enthusiasm, so instead you just keep saying, "*Wow.*" You both stare out at the corn and say it over and over until the sun finally sets and the window becomes a mirror.

You have to make it to Washington. Then—*then*—you'll be ready to talk about everything.

Outside a natural-foods store, a white woman with a mask approaches, says, "I just want to let you know that we're with you. We're all going to fight this together.

You're not alone. It's just this president, you know? He's created so much division. If we can just get him out of there, I think a lot of this could get better."

What you are capable of—on this long journey across a country in its current version of the same crisis—is a tight smile and a nod. She does most of the talking, and when her effort satisfies her need and she leaves you with a final goodbye, you're exhausted. You and your mother look at each other and roll your eyes like teenagers on vacation, shrug at a promise that "progressive" whiteness makes you every few years, every time the ghosts of their necessary evil show up to the party and make a scene too big to hide but just big enough to hide behind.

Before she ever thought to notice you, before she was ever interested, even without her, you existed.

When you're almost done for the day, almost at the pet-friendly Comfort Suites in Ogden, Utah, that you googled while you were still in Elk Mountain, Wyoming, the dust starts. Soon the air is full of sand and years of accumulating debris, and the body of the car sways suddenly, the steering wheel jolts in your mother's hands. Feeling out of control and up to your neck in unex-pressed disappointment and bad news, you grip the door handle until it hurts.

Your phone vibrates in your lap, notifies you that someone has messaged you on Instagram. From the noti-fication preview, you can see that it begins: hi. Just checking in to make sure that you're ok. i was also wondering if I could send you some of my new . . .

After every death we've managed to escape, what if it's finally the windstorm in Utah? Not the man who just can't make himself happy or domestic terrorism or the police. Not the things that I believe in or the people that I love or the way that I am. Not the toxic food or the toxic environment or the 5G. Not my mother's breast cancer diagnosis twelve years ago. Not a mechanical failure on my way to accept an award for being articulate in public. Not the money or the stress or the lack of a vacation. Not the virus. Not the president. Not the people who are only here to be right about everything. Not me. No, of course not. It's going to be the fucking windstorm in Utah. And the only thing to blame will be nature and timing. The rest we ran from in vain. It was never even meant for us. Our destiny was always leading us here, just when we were finally starting to get somewhere.

Your mother sits up straight, slows the car down to a quarter of the speed limit. You imagine that the cars that speed by in the left lane are endemic to the area, so used to sudden bouts of low visibility that their eyes have adjusted over time.

You ride in silence. When the wind finally stops, you realize that it won't kill you, and that means that every-thing else still can. You're relieved and something else, too.

"That got scary for a second. Shit," your mother says.

"I know. For me too," you say.

You both laugh, joke about the wind that almost blew you away for good.

You make it to Ogden and check into the Comfort Inn from behind the blue tape. They're using the decline in business to renovate. So, in the lobby and in the hall-ways, there are exposed wires hanging from missing ceiling tiles, carpet covered in plastic tarps. The smell of fresh white paint reminds you that you still have one more chapter left to finish of *Invisible Man*.

You'll do it when you get to Washington.

Once you are safely inside your nonsmoking double room, you take a tropical hard-candy edible and spend eighty-six dollars on two yellow curries and a side of brown rice on DoorDash and begin to unpack the essentials. Your mother calls your brother on speaker to let him know you're done driving for the day. On the second floor, it sounds like two hundred wildly enthusiastic and unattended children from the local marching band are practicing a routine for some big competition.

Your dog begins to bark at the talented children in their special steel-toe boots and you can feel your mother growing tense at the noise and you're starting to do that thing where you keep asking yourself if you're high, which means that you definitely are, and from some-where across the room your phone dings, letting you know that Justin in a white Camry is out front with your order.

Before you can figure out how to make yourself move, there is a boom quickly followed by a *hum, zap!* The room goes dark, and suddenly everything is strangely quiet, off. Across the parking lot, no one left the lights on at the Motel 6 either.

There is nothing to do but wander down the unlit hallway with your cell phone flashlight and to pry open the automatic door in the lobby to retrieve your order from Justin and ask the person at the front desk if she knows what's going on and for her to say it's lights out for half the town and for you to go back to the room and tell your mother while you quickly open flimsy containers of heavy food. And there's nothing left to do but note that the curry looks and tastes almost exactly like Campbell's vegetable soup and to ask yourself what you expected and to laugh and laugh and laugh and complain and use the complaining as a way to say a few of the things you've wanted to say for days and for your mother to go talk to the manager in that voice she's used your whole life to indicate that something or someone is about to be free, and to have the manager say, "We have two people stuck in the elevator right now, so, see? Some people here have it worse than you after all," and to have your mother come back from the front desk and tell you that you're getting moved to a newly renovated room on the second floor, where you spend the rest of the evening inhaling a fresh coat of white paint and the sweet scent of a small but necessary victory on a long but necessary day.

When you finally cross the Washington state line, you want to cry but you still can't, so you cheer instead. You stay in your brother's vacant house in Bellingham, where he and his old roommates still have two more months left on their lease. They're almost all moved out with the exception of a couple of beds, a kitchen table and chairs, and a couch.

It's a yellow house that sits across the street from a popular Thai restaurant on a short block of brightly colored houses in the desirable "Lettered Streets" district. This is the area of town where you can find coffee shops, breweries, protests, holistic veterinary care, expensive little houses covered in solar panels and prayer flags, rows and rows of lacinato kale and a line of mammoth sunflowers. At the end of the block is the ocean.

That night, you toast with a red wine blend and food from a grocery store cold case and look out at the trees. It stays light outside until almost ten o'clock and you can't believe that you had forgotten to miss that part of Washington while you were away from it.

While you're in the yellow house, you take walks around the neighborhood and say hello back to all the people who stop to ask what brought you into town.

"Are you students? No? Well, welcome anyway!"

On Thursday, your brother comes up to visit. You order too much food from across the street, and after you finish eating, you all take a walk around the neighborhood.

There are chalk memorials on the sidewalk for George Floyd and BLACK LIVES MATTER signs perched in almost every window, right next to a sleeping cat or a plant.

On your way back, you notice two white women standing in line at the Thai restaurant. One of them is staring at you, a smile slowly widening across her face. She points at each of you individually, then grabs her friend and turns her around in your direction.

"See? *See?* I told you! They *are* here!"

It plays out quickly and you almost don't believe it as it's happening, but she raises her fist in the air, starts chanting, "Black Lives Matter! Black Lives Matter! Fuck racism!"

You acknowledge her and keep walking. People are stopping on the street to see what all the fuss is about, and she uses their attention as an opportunity to rally them. "Come on, everybody! Let them know that black lives matter here!"

Her friend looks at you, smiles an apology, asks her to please stop making a scene.

As you're walking up the driveway of the yellow house, your body rigid with rage, she continues to yell after you, "*You* fucking matter! Your life fucking matters! Black Lives Fucking Matter!"

Matter: An affair or situation under consideration; a topic.

You all step into the house, close the door behind you, and through the walls you can still hear her insisting that you matter, but you don't know who she's telling, and she doesn't either.

That night, you try not to picture her. Instead, you finish *Invisible Man* with the window wide open and the sun still out. You listen to a couple fight about a cigarette that he wasn't supposed to finish but did anyway.

It feels like summer.

Do you ever think about why people unfollow you? I do. But more than that, I think about what the final straw was. Because let's be real here—if you post the exact same thing wearing the exact same T-shirt for three years, people will eventually realize you ain't shit and hit that button. And you know what? I wish those people nothing but good, seasonally appropriate joy and happiness. I do. But sometimes I *wake up* to forty-seven fewer followers. And I need y'all to tell me what happened. There you are living your life . . . using lines from Nayyirah Waheed poetry to help you recover from your latest breakup and, like, drying herbs and maybe watching reruns of *Moesha*, when all of a sudden you're like, "Uh-uh. Fuck that bitch, Jill. I'm done."

What happened, yo?!?!?!

I ain't even posted in four days and it's 5 A.M., tho!

Like, don't do that. Unfollow me in the real actual morning or in the late afternoon like you've got some damn sense. Unfollow me because I only like your photos when your mom's in them. Unfollow me because I'm always high and only sometimes making sense.

But whatever you do, don't surprise me with it. Have some decency.

Shit.

Update: To all y'all unfollowing me this afternoon, well played.

—*Jillisblack*, December 9, 2015

UNFOLLOW ME

The 2020 election is a few weeks away, and my family and I have moved to Olympia for the second time. This time, to the heavily forested outskirts of a capital city that hasn't changed nearly as quickly as we have since we left it four years ago to head back to a Deep South that's still just a little too deep for me.

After so many moves in the last few years, I have grown increasingly more uncomfortable with naming anything outside myself as a "home," worried that it will always feel like a trap or a setup. An identity too susceptible to circumstance to be an identity that I desire.

Not all trees are deeply rooted by nature. Some grow their roots close to the surface. If they're buried too far down in the dirt, growth stops, and the stress eventually kills them.

And yet, I am also happy to return to Olympia, and to remember the right streets to turn left on, and the person who still works in the alcohol and spirits department at Grocery Outlet. I see her every Monday when I drive the twenty-four minutes there from our house to buy heavily discounted, quick-sale organic kale and red wine blends straight from the southern region of Central California. I like that I recognize her even with her mask on.

The new place—with the yard that's just big enough not to intimidate and the quiet that makes me use my inside voice even when I'm standing outside, the quiet that's interrupted only by the random vocalizations of Steller's jays and northern flickers, the free-roaming long-haired cats that torment the eager short-haired dogs in fenced yards, the footsteps of the deer as they nibble their way down the fence of Taylor junipers that separate us from our new neighbor on one side, the one who waves when we see him—feels more like home than anywhere I've ever lived.

I panic. Anxious for the distraction of a calamity or a big, sudden decision that isn't about the end of my marriage or a big, sudden fight that isn't with my stepfather, or a big, sudden forward motion that isn't yet another quick move back.

I'm anxious for the chaos that doesn't surprise. The consistent one.

Luckily, I have a smart phone. It allows me to access my chaos from an outside source, fast and cheap. And by the second week, I've managed to convince myself that the other next-door neighbor (the one who has never spoken) is in some kind of angry white-pride militia. He has emphasized this level of cultural commitment by having a shaved head and several tattoos on his arms that don't seem whimsical or ironic. He also wears a concerning number of black T-shirts, the graphics made indistinguishable by the distance between us.

When he fills his hummingbird feeders with fresh nectar and doesn't make eye contact with me, I can just tell that he's the enemy. When he loads his young kids into the back seat of the family's Sea Glass Pearl Prius and it's absent of the important telltale Prius bumper stickers that I rely on to know how accepted my identities are wherever I am, it's obvious that he's plotting against us. When he mows his grass and does it in large headphones, blasting music only he can hear, I can just tell that he's not trustworthy. *And*, he does it all as if he doesn't want to be bothered.

But what's he bothered *by*, exactly? The threat of small talk or the threat of blackness? That I can't really know until I know makes me nervous, so I have to try to know as much as I can. And I have to seek out the information that confirms what I suspect.

Homie is a Proud Boy.

Luckily, every three seconds there are new articles published about the pandemic and the election and the worst year that only a few people saw coming. After reading the headlines and last paragraphs of a few of those articles, I'm feeling pretty fucking confident that the neighbor is a Proud Boy. And on election night he will emerge from his house to defend his promised land against social distancing, socialized diversity, and whatever else threatens his grip on the biggest piece of the pie in the sky.

But even if he isn't, can any of us really be too careful? What would be enough to validate my fear? Isn't all the fear valid when everything feels like a threat? If everything I hold on to might be mistaken for a weapon? If the stakes are so high that if I'm right, I just might die of it?

And I'm always trying to decide which one I'd rather be more—wrong or alive.

But I'm not wrong, right? Because militias are happening. And I'm not wrong, right? Because every time my brother goes for a run, I have to pretend that I'm not hyperaware of every long minute until he returns. And I'm not wrong, right? Because we live in a big, scary world where we control nothing and no one unless . . . well, you really can't trust anybody, honestly.

Unless they agree with you. Not only about everyone else and who they really are. But about who you really are, too.

Social media is suggesting that if I have a remote job, I should escape the United States and move somewhere safe that has really good internet connection. This way I can keep my American job and live *very* well in a country that has a lower cost of living. Plus, I don't even have to miss out on entertaining myself with the bad news from back home. It will follow me on my smart phone and make me feel included.

Something to seriously consider.

I read an article at 2 A.M. that screams its headline from the belly of my popular searches and mined data, BLACK MAN SET ON FIRE BY WHITE NEIGHBOR IN RURAL AMERICA! And even though the article eventually reveals itself to be about a lovers' quarrel over an alleged infidelity and stolen drugs, the truth of it doesn't solve my problem.

It's not about what it is. It's about what it *could have been* but happened not to be. What it *could always be*, until it is.

In the mostly white neighborhood of diverse incomes where I now live, there is a quiet war being waged. On front lawns and in the windows of houses, there are mostly small BIDEN-HARRIS, anti-Trump, and TRUST SCIENCE signs and a few large KEEP AMERICA GREAT ones, too. There are Bernie bumper stickers and faded Ben Carson ones, too. There are Tibetan prayer flags hanging from the turquoise trims of tiny houses, and there are IN THIS HOUSE WE PRAY flags in front of the slightly bigger houses, too. There are also badge-shaped security company signs highly visible in almost everyone's front yards—in case any version of God ever requires a helping hand or a little bit of backup.

I make an appointment to have a security system installed. If they all have them, then we *definitely* need one.

Every morning and every night I check the news on my phone so that I can be reminded of why I should always be scared or mad. How it's my civic duty. A way to participate.

Even though assumptions save some people's lives and end others', I figure they're my right at this point. And it's a privilege to get to *check* the news instead of being the news.

Remember that.

Perhaps the neighbor is a Proud Boy, so I must decide what I want to do about him.

But first . . .

I must finish the essay. The essay that is meant to be the last essay of this book, about Jillisblack and me these days. How we get along.

I try a lot of different versions of it, but in each version I stop just short of what I really mean. Hide it behind a breastplate of sarcasm. I don't give myself up, because I'm worried that it's not what anyone wants from me. When the truth is, I don't think Jillisblack's way of seeing everything as black or white—her way of believing that everyone who is not in agreement with her is actually in denial of themselves—works. I no longer thrive on the kind of hopelessness that she requires to get out of bed in the morning. I don't think she knows any more about anyone else than anyone else knows about *me*.

Still, I'm worried that I'm always hiding my desire in the bodies of the people I critique, holding them accountable for everything about myself that I can't yet admit to or escape from.

I'm worried that I'm like a child, always believing a game is broken and pointless once I've finished playing it. Once it's beat me.

I'm worried that I'm like Sisyphus, eternally useless and endlessly frustrated by performing a task that is a consequence of itself.

I should be writing the final essay, but instead I'm watching on the live security camera as my presumably Proud neighbor checks his mail and hides his agenda from me. Watching him reminds me of the only Jillisblack story I don't like to tell. The one I will absolutely never allow to be in the final essay of this book.

I don't tell it because I only tell the stories where I remain likable throughout or, at the very least, redeemable by humor, culture, time passed, lessons learned. Like the time I learned it was time to give Jillisblack a break from social media.

I don't tell it because that would be like scoring a point on myself for the other team. Trapping myself for the hunter.

I don't tell it because I would be admitting to the privilege of being alive long enough, potentially packaged well enough, nice-white-liberal-adjacent enough for the book deal and the edgy race-themed stories I've promised to tell—instead of the ones that promise to tell on me.

So of course I can't ever, ever, *ever* allow myself to write, "One time I got so tired of being agreed with on the internet that I had an hour-long conversation with a Proud Boy and it didn't end badly." Or, "Contrary to the popular narrative, the conversations in my DMs that ended the worst were with proud white liberal women who accused me of being ungrateful anytime my line of questioning was too unpredictable. Who were fine with everything I had to say about white people until it was about one of them. Not their new ways to be antiracist or their progressive politics or their intersectional book club or their black-and-white selfies of support, but *them*, and what they *actually* wanted from me. Not as a group of proud white liberal women, but rather as individual white women who would come into the comment section to (first) identify as proud liberals, then ask why I was so comfortable disappointing them."

I never asked the individual proud white liberal women why it is that someone screaming at them in ALL CAPS about how evil they inherently are, reducing them down to the internet definition of a "Karen," demanding that they save their unanswered questions for Google, dragging them by their Twitter fingers all across the internet and daring them to cry is found to be *absolutely brilliant! Soooooo fucking raw and real! THE TRUTH.* Met with a chorus of YOU ARE HOLDING MY MIRROR AND SHOWING ME WHO I AM! *Please tell me all about myself! Read me for everything I've done!*

I neeeeeeeeeeeeeeeeed it!!! I DESERVE IT!!! I'll be quiet so I can be seen.

I never asked what the individual proud white liberal women get from it or how they know they're learning.

If you feel like giving up, that's how you know it's working!

I never asked the individual proud white liberal women how a public flogging would lead them to greater empathy and understanding of themselves and the world around them.

I imagined the answer was that it made them feel like they were somehow doing their civic duty, participating. Or maybe because they don't find who they follow for a flogging to be capable enough, human enough, individual enough to ever be self-motivated or strategic, insecure or conflicted, needy or indulgent. Like them.

But I should've asked.

Anyway, I don't tell the one story about Jillisblack that I don't like to tell, because I'd lose and I can't lose in public. That's what gets you unfollowed.

But if I could do it without losing, I would write about the time in 2017 when I am sent a direct message that reads, "You're a fucking monkey dyke and I hope you die soon and put us all out of our misery. You dumb fucking cunt."

It's poetic enough, but I'm too tired to be moved by it. I've only been a cultural commentator on social media for a few months at this point, and already the message is too obvious to still be entertaining. I can't work up enough anger to fight him with my usual sarcasm and practiced one-liners. Especially with no one watching.

Besides, I've tried it.

I've attempted to one-up a sad person from a smart phone. I know that even when I screenshot it and repost it for the sake of the collective ego, and my following declares me the winner, it can't be true. Spending my time one-upping a sad person is a way of admitting that I'm a sad person myself.

Performing critique for public consumption and social capital has made me a person who is always a little bit sad and very, *very* anxious.

And again, I've tried it.

He's come to me as a fourteen-year-old soccer player from Berlin named Ben who enjoys the musical catalog of Wiz Khalifa and posing with his friends in front of large symbols of big masculinity and who sometimes sends me photos of dog shit that he's named after me.

<Insert five Face with Tears of Joy emoji here>

He's come to me as a lonely white dad with a trucking business who just wants to know how claiming to know everything about people I don't really know shit about is soooo fucking different when I do it, huh?

<nigger>

He's come to me as a twenty-one-year-old women's studies major named Emma who wants to know why I'm talking shit about the kind of white people who actually want to help end oppression. The patriarchy. Colonialism. Etc. Emma is an ally. Why don't I want her?

<then maybe I don't want to be your fucking ally after all bitch. good fucking luck>

The day I respond to the Proud Boy who calls me a fucking monkey dyke, I almost can't help myself. I want to know what's on the other end of the conversation that I'm never supposed to entertain. The one that neither of us supposedly deserves, but for very different reasons.

I want to talk to the primary source. I don't want everything I think I know to come from someone else. Or a documentary or a think piece or a news report or a meme or a caption or a campaign. I want it straight from the horse's shit.

Straight from the boy with all the pride.

But Jillisblack is in the room, because now she always is. And she's staring at me with that smirk, the raised eyebrow. The oversize glasses.

She says, *"Really?"* but she means, "Why do you always have to figure out how to win?"

She's right. At first, that's what it's mostly about.

I know I can't win if I do what he expects me to do. I can't win if I give him the reaction he wants. I can win only if I surprise him or if I make him surprise himself.

So instead of trying to be clever, instead of trying to convince him how well I know him and myself and everyone else, instead of blocking him, I say, "Hi. What's going on?" And he immediately asks me, "Why are you saying dumb shit?"

I sigh, because if he's going to play it like this, I'm not going to end up playing at all. We both have to be willing to defy the gravity of it.

Jillisblack reminds you, "You don't even know if he's who he says he is. All you can see is a profile photo and a bio. Your Proud Boy could be anyone—a black person who's testing your allegiance, a JV tennis star, an ex."

I ignore her because I need him to be who he says he is in order for me to win. I tell him that I'm saying what he thinks is dumb shit because I believe it. I believe that all white people are lying about how complicit they are.

But, like, yeah. Obviously.

As am I.

The thing that bothers me, inspires the necessary rage, is that they're lying about what they already know. That they actually know better than I ever could about exactly what it is they're fighting to keep. That they pretend I'm telling them something new when I'm actually only allowed to tell them the same thing over and over again, but next time with more emphasis on the personal suffering. If they keep me running around in circles, always telling them who *I* am, maybe I won't notice that they're still who they always were.

Some white people's narrative will always call for the casting of black people in the roles of villain, idiot, sucker, submissive; but also, exception, token, muse, submissive. Anything that implies actual humanity would upset the balance and crash the illusion.

That's what I tell him.

He tells me that I must be talking about some dumbass liberals, because he doesn't give a fuck about that kind of shit I'm mentioning. He just knows that he has pride in who and what he is and no one is going to tell him not to. He has to protect himself and his family from being wiped out, and black people are stupid if they don't see who the real enemy is.

He tells me that only a liberal could listen to the crap I say.

I obviously can't argue with that.

He tells me that he doesn't get it because I don't seem entirely stupid.

I tell him that it's a strange compliment.

Jillisblack says, "What the fuck are you doing? Look at how he thinks he can talk to you!" She paces circles around my room, shaking her head and mumbling under her breath about self-hatred and internalized oppression.

He tells me that he doesn't mean it as a compliment at all. If I wasn't entirely stupid, why would I believe that the government wants to help me?

I tell him that I don't.

"This is so fucking basic," Jillisblack says.

He asks why I would believe that white people would ever willingly give up power just to hand it over to someone else.

I tell him that I don't.

"Power is subjective," Jillisblack says.

He asks why I trust the media to tell people the truth about what's really happening.

I tell him that I don't.

"We're the media now," Jillisblack says.

For a moment, he types nothing.

Jillisblack sighs loudly, says, "You have a hundred unanswered messages from people who actually agree with you. People who actually like you. Well, *me*, anyway. But you're so obsessed with the trolls and the naysayers. *Why?* Why do you feel more seen when you're questioned than when you're believed?"

Maybe I'm like the proud liberal white women who crave the accusations. Maybe I think the punishment will absolve and exalt me faster than the appreciation ever could.

I tell the Proud Boy that now I want to ask him some questions about what he believes.

"You're going to fuck this up for me, aren't you?" Jillisblack asks in disbelief.

It takes him a moment to respond, but eventually he types, "Go ahead."

I ask him if he hates black people and he says that he doesn't. But he knows that white people are better and smarter than black people and that America is proof of that. He says, "That's why you won't actually leave America, right? Only America would let you say this kind of dumb shit and get away with it."

"You deserve to read that shit because you're, like, *literally* asking for it," she says.

I have all kinds of things I'd like to say back to him about what white people are actually capable of and what America is actually proof of, but I want him to keep saying more and more of what he means.

I want him to say everything I think he'll say. I don't want to be surprised.

I ask him if he thinks white liberals are better and smarter than black people, too, and he says that he does. Because liberals lie to black people and talk shit behind their backs, and black people still trust them.

Jillisblack laughs.

I ask him if he's happy believing what he believes and he says, "That's a weird question, but sure."

I ask because it's hard to spend every moment in reaction to someone or something else. I wonder if I'm happy. Calling out, telling off, staying ready for everyone so that I never get caught off guard.

I ask him what it is that he needs to say to black people so badly that he's come into my inbox to say it to someone who so obviously disagrees with him. He says that in some ways, he gets it. Because he believes in white pride, he understands why black people would have black pride, too. That makes sense. He just doesn't approve of the way we're going about showing it. And if we keep blaming white people for all our problems, we'll keep having problems we can't fix for ourselves.

Oh, and if we keep believing white liberals actually care about us.

"Aren't you just blaming black people and liberals for all of *your* problems?" I ask him aloud in my room.

"Tell him that. Type *that!*" Jillisblack says, sitting next to me on the futon, jabbing at the screen with her index finger.

Instead, I ask him if he believes in anything bigger than whiteness, and he says that he doesn't believe in God, if that's what I mean. He says that God is another lie that people believe in just so they can feel better about their fucked-up lives.

I tell him that people believe in all kinds of things to feel better about their fucked-up lives.

He agrees.

We go back and forth until there is finally a lag between messages and it's a conversation that seems to be over. But after I've exited the app and sat still on my floor staring at the wall to avoid the screen and her gaze, and after I've started the work of avoiding an answer to the question of why I've done something so unallowed to get some answers I could've predicted, he sends another message.

"Don't open that," she warns.

I open it and hope he calls me a name so that I can get what I deserve, pay for my mistake sooner rather than later. But he doesn't. Instead, he thanks me.

He didn't expect me to respond like I did.

He gets lonely knowing all the stuff he knows about how the world really is.

He's sorry he called me those names.

He was just mad about what I was saying.

And he still is, by the way.

But he hopes I have a good rest of my day.

I make it all much worse than it has to be by not using this as an opportunity to tell him that I didn't mean any of it. That it was all just a clever trick to get him to apologize to me. Then at least I could still screenshot it, post it on my Instagram, laugh with everyone about how I fooled him, bested him. I could both indulge the conversation *and* use it to win.

I'd win.

But I don't.

I don't know what part of all the things that I am and all the apologies I've learned to give makes me want to not be rude just because he said it first. It doesn't make any sense. But I tell him thank you like it's about having good manners.

"You're self-hating as fuck right now, you know that? Do you know that you're the problem? Who needs white people when we've got you?" Jillisblack says from behind her glasses, suddenly back on the other side of the room.

I tell him that I hope he reconsiders how he feels.

"YOU *HOPE* HE *RECONSIDERS*? Are you trying to convince a supposed Proud Boy—who is definitely a sophomore at somebody's high school—to save money by bundling his cable and internet? Is that what this is? Is that why you'd be using a weak-ass word like 'reconsider'?!"

And he says, "Same to you," with a heart emoji, and that's that.

It doesn't climax with a callout. There is no follow-up story or public consequence. I try to forget about it and go back to making my weekly one-minute rants like it never happened. Like I didn't make it happen.

But Jillisblack knows, and she finds a way to tell everyone. Soon the "Dear White People" videos that she's become known for turn to "Dear Black People" ones instead.

Every single one is about a black person who says one thing but justifies another.

A black person who is an accomplice in a crime against themselves.

A black person who says "Thank you" in private and "Fuck them" in public.

A liar.

I know she's trying to get under my skin.

One time I accidentally tell another person about it. I am a little bit too high to stop myself and it slips out, lands heavily in the middle of our conversation.

"Wait, I don't get it, though," they say, looking confused and perhaps suspicious, "Why did you even talk to this guy at all?"

I try to explain, but no matter what I say, I can't make their eyes less narrow. I can't fix their frown.

I had a conversation *with* a Proud Boy instead of about one.

On purpose.

And I should know better. Because I'm me.

But more importantly, I'm Jillisblack. And even when I, Jill Louise Busby, haven't been understood as someone you can trust to not get played/suckered/bamboozled/hoodwinked, she *has*.

Maybe that's why I'm slowly allowing her to run my entire life. Maybe I think she's better at it.

Until now.

Three days before the election and twenty-five days before the first deadline for what will soon be this book, I realize where all this is going. I realize that I'm looking out the window at a sign that it's time to reveal a truth that doesn't declare me the winner. It's time to tell the whole thing.

Or the book isn't really mine.

It's hers.

I have to write it knowing that Jillisblack would read this essay and raise her right (my left) eyebrow in judgmental contempt, smirk and shrug and say, "How much did they pay you for writing this? No, really. Come on. How did they get to you? What did it take?"

She would say that she wasn't surprised, actually. That she could see this coming a million miles away from someone like me.

She didn't have to know me to know my type.

She would ask, "Did you figure out that other people were getting more popular than you and decide to pull the old switcheroo? Is this the new lane since the other one has gotten so, so very crowded?"

Was this easier to package up and sell to the highest bidder?

Can you not get mad enough anymore now that you've stopped running and you're writing the last essay of the book and you've moved into a neighborhood where you're just as worried to feel safe as you are to feel scared?

And she deserves answers.

If she were really here, able to read the words as herself and not through me, I would give them to her. Call her out by name the way she likes. Say, "Hi, Jillisblack. I miss you, too. You came into my life and answered questions I didn't even know I had. You caught me in lies I didn't even know I was telling. And you exist only on an app, a new world given to us so that we give in to a new world. It makes sense that you think you know everything and everyone. But you mistake preaching to the choir with speaking gospel truth. You think that all that you see and all that you say is all that there is. But it's just one account, and it isn't even firsthand. And to answer your question, nothing has been as easy to package up and sell as you were."

But in the end, this isn't an essay about Jillisblack or the "Proud Boy" who introduces himself and his wife a week later, tells us they've been meaning to run over to say hello, says we should holler if we ever need anything.

I could've been right about him. But so far, I wasn't.

It's not about a white liberal either. Or an election or a neighborhood. Fear or fact. It isn't an essay about who's right or wrong or who agrees or doesn't.

It's also not an essay about how Proud Boys are harmless lonely lovers of heart emojis, waiting to be engaged by indulgent social media personalities before reconsidering their choices.

That would be silly.

It's just an essay about what happened a few weeks ago.

One that I will never allow to be the last essay of this book.

*

*

*

AFTER A LONG hiatus, she starts showing up again. Looking desperate and scared like she knows the end is near for her.

"You're really going to end with the essay about the Proud Boy, huh? So you don't want the opportunity to write a second book, I guess. That's probably smart."

I look up one Monday in February and she is sitting on the edge of my bed, her back straight, her smile knowing. But I notice right away that she is due for a haircut.

"The only other option was to lead with it," I say, typing these words, sipping from a mug of black coffee gone cold.

"*Oh!* Bold choice that would've been," she mocks, "starting with a defense mechanism."

"That's not what the essay is."

"Oh, sure. Of course."

She stares at me, my fingers as they move over the keyboard

"I don't think you have enough followers to get away with this. Like, you're not famous enough to pull off having a conversation with your online persona. Because this is already kind of a 'memoir-in-essays' thing, right? *Right?* And you're only micro-famous, right? *Right?*"

I nod.

"Right. Bold choices."

I resume typing, trying to refuse her the attention she requires.

"You should let me write the book. That's the book people want. Look, once I'm undone, you can't go back. I can always be you, but you can never be me again.

Think about it. You want to write a book in a few years once everything . . . Fine, okay. No problem. But this moment is mine. It's the perfect time for what I do.

"You can't do what you do without me. You don't have your own ideas. You can't speak for yourself. That's not even your real face. You're filtered with thirty-five percent intensity Ludwig, contrasted, highlighted. I dress you. I get your hair cut."

She narrows her eyes at me. Says, "You'll miss me, you know. During an interview that goes left. When they ask why you doubt the intentions of white liberals in silly ties or white women who grin and stare. When they compare you to someone else who looks like you but who doesn't agree with you. When they ask you to explain how that could even be possible. You'll want me to do it. You'll wish I were in the room."

She's not wrong. She's an instinct. A history. A reaction. A weapon. She's a fight that's still in me, because it's not yet my initial instinct to relax, lower my shoulders, my eyebrow, my guard.

"They'll disagree with you," she warns.

"That makes sense."

"They'll ask about me."

"I want them to."

"They'll wish the book were mine, instead."

"The ones who do always did."

"Can we at least take the conversation about Beyoncé out of 'A Friend of Men'?"

"No."
"But it's a bad idea."
"I know."
"Tell them that it wasn't mine."
"Done."

ACKNOWLEDGMENTS

Thank you to Alma, Chris, and Joseline. For coffee-time realizations, celebrity gossip, book club, improv dance parties, hot water for tea, flute duets to Tamia songs, letters, loyalty, humor, and accountability. You are my best friends and the home of my most honest self. I love you like whoa.

Thank you to the Rhode Island Writers Colony. For the phone call that made it happen. For Ms. Dianne. For John. For the care and the aftercare. For the question "What are you waiting for?" For the Del's lemonade and Donny Hathaway. For Brook Stephenson. For existing.

Thank you to Jason Reynolds, Darnell Moore, and Michael Render.

Thank you to Katie Kotchman. For that initial conversation. For getting it right away. For the emails about that one reality show. For signing off with that infamous "All best." For every single thing you did to make this book possible.

Thank you to Callie Garnett. For the excitement. For the real questions. For the thoughtful pauses. For the patience and the push. For the postcard. For the kombucha jokes. For being so, so good at what you do. For bringing so, so much to this book.

Thank you to the team at Bloomsbury. You've all been amazing and working with you has been an even better experience than I could've ever imagined.

Thank you to my friends.

Thank you to the people who listened to my long, rambling WhatsApp notes about this process and, for whatever reason, didn't immediately block me. Thank you to all the early readers who took their job seriously enough to offer true feedback and necessary perspective. Thank you to the first person who read this entire thing and gave me my first review. It made me cry on the low but you didn't need to know that until now. Getting to share this with you was one of the very best parts of the journey.

Thank you to the Bolsters. I could not have written this book without your support.

Thank you to Joe Henry and Christina Fisher.

Thank you to the people I don't name anymore but who were part of making this happen.

Thank you to everyone I found online and who found me online, who shared my words or left a comment or liked a video or drove or took the subway to some event. Thank you for reading and listening. Thank you for calling me out when it made sense. Most of the time, it did. Thank you for always surprising me with the seemingly infinite boundaries of your support.

Thank you for reading this book. I kind of can't believe that you did, whoever you are. I hope that you enjoyed it or hated it or recognized yourself in it or wanted to throw it into a deep body of water and forget about it forever. I'm honored by any and all of those. Not equally, but still. THANK YOU.

And an extra special thank you to Omarion. Obviously.

A NOTE ON THE AUTHOR

JILL LOUISE BUSBY (also known as Jillisblack) had spent nearly ten years in the nonprofit sector specializing in diversity and inclusion when she uploaded to Instagram a one-minute incisive attack on liberal gradualism and the so-called progressive nonprofit machine. The video went viral, receiving millions of views across social platforms and making her the "it" voice for all things race-based and indulgently honest. Over the next few years, she amassed a loyal following of over eighty thousand people. She continues to use social media, writing, and film to expose contradictions, challenge performative authenticity, and campaign for accountability. She lives in Olympia, Washington.